# Tell Me A

# Texas Story

BOOKS BY JUNE RAYFIELD WELCH

*A Family History*   1966
*The Texas Courthouse*  1971
*Texas: New Perspectives*  1971
*Historic Sites Of Texas*  1972
*Dave's Tune*   1973
*People And Places In The Texas Past*  1974
*And Here's To Charley Boyd*  1975
*The Glory That Was Texas*  1975
*Going Great In The Lone Star State*  1976
*The Texas Governor*  1977
*The Texas Senator*  1978
*All Hail The Mighty State*  1979
*The Colleges Of Texas* 1981
*Riding Fence*  1983
*The Texas Courthouse Revisited* 1984
*A Texan's Garden Of Trivia*  1985

# Tell Me A Texas Story

## June Rayfield Welch

YELLOW
R·O·S·E
P·R·E·S·S

Copyright 1991

by

June Rayfield Welch

Library of Congress Catalog Card Number
91-65284

ISBN number 0-912854-16-2

First printing April 1991

Published by
Yellow Rose Press
Dallas, Texas

Printed by
Davis Brothers Publishing Company
Waco, Texas

# TABLE OF CONTENTS

## CHARACTERS

## COLLEGES

## COUNTIES

## EVENTS

## GOVERNORS AND PRESIDENTS

## HEROES

## SAM HOUSTON

## LEGENDS

## LIFE IN TEXAS

For Lynda,
good wife and companion,
who made this book possible.

# INTRODUCTION

In June of 1983, I began my daily "Vignettes of Texas History" series on KRLD radio. It was part of an ambition to share with Texans more of the history of their state than most had encountered.

The stories I told on those broadcasts were sufficiently numerous that, without adding new ones, it took about a year to complete a loop. Along the way, I decided that the pieces deserved greater exposure than that.

During the seven and a half years, some listeners asked if the stories were in book form. That was the only provocation I required to launch this volume, so here are ninety-eight tales from the "Vignettes of Texas History" series.

I am grateful to Ann Huey Bishop for the dust jacket and page design, to Bill Shirley and Cyndi Wendt Sykora, at Davis Brothers, for guidance, and to my wife, Lynda, for editing. As ever, I am beholden to Sister Frances Marie Manning for editorial assistance. (By pure coincidence, Richard Hill — whose letter to a brother in Kentucky appears on page 179 — was Sister Frances Marie's great grandfather.)

June Rayfield Welch

Dallas

# JONAS HARRISON OWNED A WALKING CANE

Jonas Harrison was a well-loved East Texas citizen. Harrison County — Marshall is the seat of government — was named for him. Born in New Jersey during the American Revolution, he settled in present Shelby County, Texas, where he was alcalde of the Tenaha District in 1828. Active in the Texas Revolution, Harrison died soon after independence was won.

Harrison was a very ugly man. (Ugliness was a favorite topic of frontier humor. Towns held ugly man contests, and a candidate for governor declared that there were three terribly ugly men in Texas: he was one and his opponent was the other two.

When George Pendleton appeared before a Democratic convention to accept nomination as lieutenant governor, a delegate — appalled by Pendleton's homeliness — shouted, "It's a good thing we nominated you before we saw you.")

Once, in the old states, a well-dressed man stopped Harrison on the street and gave him a handsome walking cane. He thanked the stranger, who then explained the reason for his gift: "I always believed I was the ugliest man in the world. But I am a beauty compared to you."

Although he was stung by the criticism, Harrison again expressed his gratitude, for he had never seen such a fine walking stick. The benefactor added, "There is one condition. Should you ever meet anyone uglier than you are, you must give him the cane and tell him the reason for the gift."

So Jonas Harrison went away, smarting under the stranger's criticism but rejoicing in the new possession. Through the years, he kept the stick polished and free of nicks. Then, one Saturday, on the public square in Shelbyville, Texas, Harrison met the ugliest human he had ever imagined. Harrison introduced himself, presented the cane to the ugly man, then explained his motivation.

And the new owner whipped Jonas Harrison with the walking stick.

# DAN WAGGONER WAS A SLOW MAN WITH A DOLLAR

$T$hree buildings stand above Decatur. Downtown is the grand old Wise County courthouse. To the South is the Decatur Baptist College building that has housed a museum since the institution moved away and became Dallas Baptist University. East of the railroad tracks sits the old Dan Waggoner mansion.

Many stories were inspired by the cattle-baron Waggoners. Dan founded the dynasty, and his son and partner, W. T., expanded it. Dan's second wife was a daughter of Electious Halsell. W. T. married his stepmother's sister. They all lived in the big house overlooking Decatur.

Dan Waggoner — "a little round-headed feller," according to my aunt, Rebecca Owens Hall — was notoriously slow with a dollar. Tales preserved in my family include reminiscences about Dan's habit of parking his cigar stub on a fence post outside my great grandmother's boarding house, to be reclaimed after dinner.

When Dan Waggoner was asked to contribute to a church building fund, he took $6 from his wallet and handed it over. The deeply disappointed preacher sputtered and then burst out, "You must give more than that. Your own son pledged $5,000."

Waggoner answered, "That may be, but you must remember that my son has a very rich daddy."

—

Once, W. T. was the victim of train robbers, who were furious upon discovering that he was carrying no cash. When Waggoner offered to write a check, the outraged bandit chief exploded. He warned that Waggoner better have more than $2 or $3 on his person if ever again he rode a train they chose to rob.

—

W. T. Waggoner and good friend Samuel Burk Burnett left their marks on North and West Texas. (In the time when Fort Worth was the capital of the cattle kingdom, office buildings bore the names of Burk Burnett and both Waggoners. Burkburnett, in Wichita County, is near Electra, which bears the name of W. T.'s daughter.)

But neither Burnett nor W. T. Waggoner was a significant intellectual, spiritual, or cultural force. One night they fell to arguing religion, and Burnett claimed to possess a superior knowledge of the Bible. Waggoner then bet $100 that Burnett could not recite the Lord's Prayer.

Burnett accepted the wager, ruminated briefly, and declaimed, "Now I lay me down to sleep. I pray the Lord my soul to keep ...."

And Waggoner paid the $100 bet.

—

# CARRY NATION WAS A NUISANCE IN RICHMOND

As a girl, Kentucky-born Carry Moore moved to a Grayson County, Texas farm. The livestock died, and after typhoid claimed some slaves, her father freed the rest and took his family to Missouri.

Carry's marriage, at age nineteen, to an alcoholic physician caused her to develop strong feelings against liquor. After the doctor's death, she married David Nation, a lawyer-preacher almost twenty years her senior. They had a tough time, due partly to Carry's desire to reform everyone and everything.

In 1879, the Nations moved to a Brazoria County farm where, knowing nothing about farming, they nearly starved. David Nation's attempt to practice law in Columbia met with little success. In desperation, Carry rented an old hotel building and, with $3.50 of borrowed capital, began renting rooms.

A nuisance in Columbia and Richmond—where she persisted in trying to improve the world — Carry received little gratitude for her good work.

In Richmond, Nation took sides in Fort Bend County's political wars between the Jaybirds and Woodpeckers and was badly beaten. He and Carry moved to Medicine Lodge, Kansas about 1890.

Each time Nation preached, Carry supervised from a front row pew. Her assistance included on-the-spot suggestions, and should she decide the sermon was not going well, Carry would announce, "That will be all, David." If Nation failed to obey, she would invade the pulpit, slam the Bible shut, stuff his hat onto his head, and order him to go home.

As Carry Nation took personal charge of the war against alcoholic beverages, she earned a national reputation by brandishing a hatchet, wrecking saloons, and assaulting bartenders.

She signed her letters, "Your loving home defender."

—

Nation, Carry A., The Use and Need of the Life of Carry A. Nation, Topeka: Steves, 1904.

# CARRY NATION INVADED THE UNIVERSITY OF TEXAS

As the twentieth century approached, Carry Nation was trying to purify Kansas, where the sale of intoxicants was prohibited by law. In Medicine Lodge, she invaded the business establishments that served hard liquor. At nearby Kiowa she threw bricks at the mirrors and bottles in Dobson's Saloon. (Dobson retreated into a corner.) After destroying three other places and defying the Kiowa officials who threatened to arrest her, Carry rode away, shouting, "Peace on earth. Goodwill to men."

Mrs. Nation was not the sweet little old lady she appeared to be at first glance. She was about six feet tall and weighed 180 pounds. Gentlemen did not know how to defend themselves against her. When arrested for wrecking some Wichita saloons, she slapped the sheriff repeatedly and dragged him by the ears until he was rescued by a policeman.

By 1901, Mrs. Nation was organizing the National Hatchet Brigade and publishing a newspaper, The Smasher's Mail. Arrested frequently, she financed her legal expenses and the campaign against strong drink by the sale of toy hatchets.

While smashing New York City saloons, Carry Nation was summoned to Austin because of an emergency at the University of Texas. Law students reported that their high morals were jeopardized by depraved, drunken, and licentious professors.

On October 16, 1902 — accompanied by cheering students — Carry strode into an Austin alderman's saloon. She brandished her hatchet, and he threw her out.

Mrs. Nation then invaded the campus of the state university. As delighted students identified professors and detailed accusations, she snatched cigars and pipes from the mouths of distinguished and superannuated scholars and judges. Denouncing the learned gentlemen, she demanded that they mend their ways and stop corrupting Texas youth.

In a 1904 rematch, students charged beloved Dean T. U. Taylor — a Sunday School superintendent for many years — with being "the worst reprobate at the University." A witness recalled that,

> Carry came sailing toward Dean Taylor ... [shouting] "You old booze hound. You are the leader of these innocent boys and get them to join this drunken ... crowd." All twenty of the boys that were with her were yelling, "That's right, Mrs. Nation."

Carry Nation was defeated in her last battle as she tried to destroy a nude painting displayed in Mary Maloy's Dance Hall and Cafe in Butte, Montana. During the altercation, someone broke a chair over Mrs. Nation's head. She died a few months later.

—

Nation, Carry A., The Use and Need of the Life of Carry A. Nation, Topeka: Steves, 1904.

# WILLIAMSON WAS "THREE-LEGGED WILLIE"

In his fifteenth year, Robert M. Williamson suffered a debilitating illness that rendered useless the lower part of his right leg. With the maimed limb strapped up behind him, he walked on a wooden leg. While recuperating, "Three-Legged Willie" studied law, and, at age eighteen, he was admitted to the Georgia bar.

After fighting a duel over a young lady who had married a rival, in 1826, Williamson came to Texas. At San Felipe he edited The Cotton Plant, a newspaper he owned with G. B. Cotten. (A huge, portly man, Cotten enjoyed being questioned about his initials, so he could respond, "What do they stand for? Can't you see? Great Big, of course.")

The Cotton Plant went broke, and Williamson began devoting himself to the law; however, he was active enough in politics that Mexican authorities tried to arrest him. He served in the cavalry at the battle of San Jacinto.

As judge of the Republic's third circuit, Williamson held court where there had never been any formal administration of justice. In Colorado County, he tried cases beneath a great oak tree in the absence of a courthouse. (Badly damaged by pollution, time, and lightning, the tree still stood in the middle of a Columbus street a few years ago.)

Settlers were not always thrilled by the imposition of law and order, and Judge Williamson was as tough as he had to be. In one sullen and hostile community, "Three-Legged Willie" unpacked the law books from his saddlebags, sat down behind a table he would use as a bench, laid a pistol and a rifle beside a roll of pleadings, and announced, "Hear ye! Hear ye! Court for the third district is either now in session or somebody's going to get killed."

—

Robinson, Duncan, Judge Robert McAlpin Williamson: Texas' Three-Legged Willie, 1949.

Smithwick, Noah, The Evolution of a State, Austin: Steck-Vaughn Company, 1968.

# JUDGE WILLIAMSON ESTABLISHED RESPECT FOR THE LAW

Old settler Noah Smithwick wrote that nature, in the case of Robert M. Williamson,

> ... had indeed been lavish of her mental gifts, but as if repenting of her prodigality in that line, she later afflicted him with a grievous physical burden; his right leg being drawn up at a right angle at the knee, necessitating the substitution of a wooden leg, which circumstance gave rise to the name by which he was familiarly known — "Three-Legged Willie."

Judge Williamson "would leave a courtroom over which he had just presided with all the grace and dignity of a lord chief justice, and within an hour be patting Juba for some nimble-footed scapegrace to dance."

Early one morning, at San Felipe, blacksmith Smithwick, was aroused by someone calling, "O Smithwick; come here; here's a man with a broken leg."

Smithwick opened his door and found Williamson sitting on the porch. His wooden leg was damaged from a night of celebration. "I took the fractured limb to my shop and braced it up so that it was as good as new, and the Judge went on his way rejoicing."

A strong advocate of Texas' joinder to the United States, Williamson named a son Annexus.

"Three-Legged Willie" established respect for the law in a fashion that was well understood by frontiersmen. He asked a drunken lawyer who was arguing a case, "Where is the law to support your position?"

Brandishing a Bowie knife, the attorney replied, "There's the law."

Judge Williamson unholstered his pistol, aimed at a wrinkle midway between the lawyer's eyebrows, and said, "Yes, and here's the Constitution."

—

Robinson, Duncan, Judge Robert McAlpin Williamson: Texas' Three-Legged Willie, 1949.

Smithwick, Noah, The Evolution of a State, Austin: Steck-Vaughn Company, 1968.

# IKE PRYOR FELL VICTIM TO HIS OWN GOOD ADVICE

J. Marvin Hunter published some marvelous tales he had heard from old trail drivers. One concerned a character reference Ike Pryor wrote for an Indian chief — probably in an attempt to get rid of him.

In the 1870s, Pryor drove a herd up the Chisholm Trail to Kansas a few days ahead of Bill Jackman's outfit. It was customary for drovers to catch stray cattle they found along the road and to keep them until they could be restored to their owners.

In the Indian Territory, a Jackman cowhand brought in a steer that wore Pryor's brand. Jackman was taking the animal to the railhead for return to Pryor when, one day, a band of about forty Indians, who seemed to be spoiling for trouble, rode up to the chuck wagon. The impatient and overbearing chief demanded that a steer be given to him; he handed Jackman a note which read,

To the trail bosses:

This man is a good Indian; I know him personally. Treat him well. Give him a beef and you will have no trouble in driving through his country.

Ike Pryor

Jackman sent a man to the chuck wagon to get his glasses. He studied the message at length, showed it to a couple of cowhands, sighed, and rode into the herd. Jackman cut out the Pryor steer and delivered it to the chief.

With dancing and singing remembered from buffalo-hunting days, the Indians slaughtered the steer and began preparing for a feast. Jackman hurried northward with his own herd intact — rejoicing, and grateful for Ike Pryor's sound advice.

—

Hunter, J. Marvin, Ed., <u>Trail Drivers of Texas</u>, Nashville: Cokesbury Press, 1925.

# JUANA CAVASOS BARNARD WAS A COMANCHE CAPTIVE

Through his trading posts, Charles Barnard made important contributions to the development of Texas. One historian stated that he was better known than "any other individual of his time, due to his many good deeds done to help both the pioneers and the Indians, and his influence in keeping peace between the races."

The girl who became Barnard's wife, Juana Cavasos, was captured by the Comanche near Matamoras in 1843. She never saw her parents again.

Three years later, the Indians traded the Spanish-Italian captive for supplies at Barnard's trading post, near the Waco Indian village. Barnard and Juana married in 1848. Their dozen boys and two girls included three sets of twins, and John Barnard was the first white child born in Hood County.

Mrs. Barnard was reunited with her twin brother, Juan, when his trail herd, bound for Dodge City, stopped overnight near Barnard's Hood County trading house. He told Mrs. Barnard that their parents were dead. Juan Cavasos farmed in Hood County for many years.

By two-seated surrey, Juana Cavasos Barnard traveled to Matamoras in search of surviving kinsmen. Her grandson, Burl Barnard, said,

> There were few roads at the time; they made their way by guess-work and good luck. They found two of her brothers still living there. These brothers later moved near the Barnard Trading Post at Fort Spunky.

He added,

> My grandmother, who lived to be eighty years of age, was an expert swimmer and horsewoman. She traveled by horseback via sidesaddle until the day she died with a stroke.

Juana Cavasos Barnard died February 1, 1906.

—

Andrus, Pearl, Juana, Waco: 1982.

Ewell, Thomas T., A History of Hood County, Texas, Granbury: 1895.

Granbury Junior Woman's Club, Hood County in Picture and Story, Fort Worth: Historical Publications, 1978.

# TOM BEAN WAS FANNIN COUNTY'S RICH MAN

---

Tom Bean, a leading Fannin County citizen in the last century, had a blue eye and a brown eye and was the richest man in Bonham.

Beginning his working life as a surveyor, Bean accumulated enough land that some claimed — and believed — that he could ride from Bonham to Austin without getting off his own property.

No one knew much about Bean. Always well dressed, he wore a silk vest, tweed trousers, a stiff-collared white shirt, and highly-polished boots. Bean was invariably kind and dignified. The fact that he had never married caused Bean to be especially interesting to women. He lived in a poor neighborhood and was master of the Masonic lodge. He made substantial contributions to several Bonham churches, but he did not join one.

After Bean's death, in 1887, dozens of claimants tried to show reasons why they should inherit his estate. In the end, none proved their kinship, and, apparently, the land escheated to the state.

Fannin County historian Floy Hodge told of Bean's unfortunate experience at the close of worship services one Sunday evening. The preacher had extended the invitation and had been rewarded by some conversions. A lady who took a special interest in the state of Bean's soul sat down beside him and urged that he respond to the minister's invitation. As Mrs. Hodge put it, the

> ... buxom woman quivered by his side and said, "Oh, Colonel Bean, don't you want to go to heaven?"

The quiet gentleman bowed with his usual courtly grace and said, "Well, not tonight, ma'am, not tonight."

—

The Grayson County town that bears his name had a population of 926 in 1980. Its high school athletic teams compete as the Tom Bean Tom Cats.

—

Hodge, Floy, A History of Fannin County, Hereford: Pioneer Publishers, 1966.

# HANK SMITH BUILT THE FIRST HOUSE ON THE PLAINS

Henry Clay Smith — the South Plains' first permanent settler — was born Heinrich Schmitt, in Germany. A former seaman, a teamster who hauled freight over the Santa Fe Trail, a cowboy, and a gold miner, as he decided to settle down Smith sold hay to the Army at Fort Griffin. In Shackelford County, Texas, he met and married Elizabeth Boyle, a native of Scotland.

Smith contracted to build a ranch house in present Crosby County in 1876. The lumber was to be hauled by ox wagon from Fort Worth. His principal defaulted, and Smith finished and occupied the house. It was the first permanent home — the original center of civilization — on the Plains.

"Uncle Hank" dug the first water well on the Plains, planted the first crop, and set out the first orchard. Mrs. Smith — "Aunt Hank" — doctored the ill and injured until a physician moved to the county. She was the first, and only, postmistress, or postmaster, at Mount Blanco.

Crosby County was created in 1876 and was placed under Baylor County's jurisdiction until it attained sufficient voters to organize. The Quaker Paris Cox founded Estacado shortly before the 1880 census showed Crosby's population to be about 50 souls.

Smith carried a petition through ten unorganized counties to obtain the 150 signatures needed to establish a government for Crosby County. He accepted the assistance of "Quakers, Gentiles, Philistines, transients, buffalo hunters, and just anybody who would sign." Smith then rode three days to present the petition to Baylor County's commissioners at Seymour.

As Crosby County's first tax assessor, Smith was denied reelection because he had done his job too efficiently. He and "Aunt Hank" are buried at the abandoned town of Emma, and a replica of their home stands in downtown Crosbyton.

—

Burgess, Roger Andrew, "The History of Crosby County, Texas," Master of Arts thesis, University of Texas, 1927.

# WALTER CHRYSLER MADE HIS OWN TOOLS

From boyhood, Walter Chrysler was fascinated by machinery. After graduation from high school, he worked as a nickel-an-hour apprentice mechanic in the Union Pacific Railroad shops. Following custom, Chrysler made his own set of tools.

As master mechanic of the Fort Worth and Denver City Railway, Chrysler was ordered to rebuild the West Texas equipment maintenance facilities. The Clarendon shops had burned, and the replacement buildings were to be located at Childress. Chrysler's early reputation was based upon his performance in constructing those shops.

Chrysler found only one house available for rent at Childress. It stood in a cornfield, and drinking water had to be hauled in, but the rent was only $10 a month.

Chrysler bought his first automobile in 1908. He dismantled the car and tinkered for three months before teaching himself to drive.

Chrysler was working for the American Locomotive Company when Charles Nash hired him to run the Buick factory. The new assembly line installed by Chrysler increased production from forty-five to two hundred Buicks per day.

Because of his growing reputation, Chrysler was retained to make the Willys-Overland Company profitable again. Then he contracted to salvage the Maxwell Company, which, in the end, became the Chrysler Corporation.

Walter Chrysler's engineers designed a new car which would bear his name. He bought the Dodge Brothers' company and began manufacturing Plymouths. By 1937, the Chrysler Corporation was producing six thousand cars a day.

Later, ruminating upon the tools he had taken to Childress and finally deposited in New York City, Chrysler wrote,

> Years after I ceased to need them to earn a living those tools ... [were] placed on display in a glass case on the observatory floor seventy-one stories up in the tower of the Chrysler Building. There, on a clear day, a visitor may look to a horizon nearly forty miles away .... Yet I am sure that one who neglects the view to gaze, with understanding, into that chest of tools I made, will have learned more about America than one who looks from an observatory window down into the uneven mass of steel, stone and brick that forms the city.

—

Chrysler, Walter P., Life of an American Workman, New York: Dodd, Mead, 1937.

# CHARLES POST DEVISED A COFFEE SUBSTITUTE

In 1886, Charles W. Post suffered a breakdown which caused him to move from the Midwest to Fort Worth to improve his health. He lived near present Forest Park and helped develop the Sylvania Addition. When Post's health failed again, he was sent to the Seventh Day Adventist Sanitarium, in Battle Creek, Michigan. It was a most fortunate illness.

Post's recovery was accelerated by his desire to escape the dietary restrictions imposed upon patients. The Adventists were vegetarians and did not permit coffee or tea. The superintendent, Dr. John Kellogg, and his brother, business manager W. K. Kellogg, did offer grain substitutes for the prohibited coffee, but Post believed he could devise a more palatable drink. He knew poor West Texas farmers who brewed, from chicory and roasted wheat, a better product than the sanitarium served its patients.

After his release from the hospital, Post remained in Battle Creek. Working in his barn workshop, he concocted a coffee substitute of wheat, bran, and molasses that he named Postum. In 1895, he sold the first Postum at Grand Rapids. Three years later, Post's sales were almost a million dollars per annum.

The second product, Grape Nuts, helped make Post a millionaire. Not until he brought out Elijah's Manna did he have a failure, but that problem was solved by changing the name to Post Toasties.

While he was in the process of building Post City, in Garza County, Charles Post died in 1914. His only child, Marjorie Meriwether Post, and her husband, E. F. Hutton, bought the Jell-O Company, Swans Down Cake Flour, and Minute Tapioca and began expanding the Postum Company into General Foods Corporation.

—

Eaves, Charles and Hutchinson, C. A., <u>Post City, Texas</u>, Austin: The Texas State Historical Association, 1952.

Wright, William, <u>Heiress</u>, Washington, D. C.: New Republic Books, 1978.

# LAWYER GRAY FOLLOWED THE CIRCUIT "FOOTBACK AND WALKING"

Among the eccentric lawyers who practiced in early Texas was "Walking" Gray, of Beaumont, who traveled the five- or six-county circuit with other attorneys, but while they rode from courthouse to courthouse, Gray made the tour — as Texans used to put it —"footback and walking."

—

Because of their notorious ineptitude, two criminal lawyers in Gainesville were known locally as the "penitentiary agents."

—

Since he had no partner, Panhandle attorney W. H. Woodman referred to himself as "The Lone Wolf of Yellow House Canyon." He claimed to be "English by birth, Virginian by education, and Texan by the grace of God." Instead of studying law books, Woodman listened to — and remembered — the legal points made by other barristers. An able speaker, Woodman persuaded juries more times than not.

—

Soon after Millie Jones Porter's family arrived in Mobeetie, her brother got sick. Her father — dead broke — begged for credit to buy the medicine the boy needed, but the druggist was a newcomer who was unfamiliar with the trust the people of the Plains extended to each other. The merchant refused to charge the $2 purchase, although the desperate father offered his $40 horse as security. Finally, lawyer Lorenzo Dow Miller — who had heard the entire conversation — stated, "Aw, let him have the medicine. If he never pays, I will."

Years later, Mrs. Porter was clerking in a store when Miller's wife came in to buy a Christmas present for her husband. Mrs.

Porter suggested a wallet, but Mrs. Miller declined. Smiling ruefully, she explained that her husband "gave his money away before it had time to reach his wallet."

—

Porter, Millie Jones, <u>Memory Cups of Panhandle Pioneers</u>, Clarendon: Clarendon Press, 1945.

# TEMPLE HOUSTON GAVE HIS BEST ADVICE

Temple Lea Houston, the youngest son of "old Sam Jacinto," was the first child born in the Governors Mansion at Austin. The most colorful of Houston's children, he stood well over six feet in height, wore his hair shoulder-length, and sported a rattlesnake hatband. Sometimes, Temple Houston strapped on six-shooters, and he was rumored to have bested such gunmen as William "Billy the Kid" Bonney and "Bat" Masterson in shooting contests.

A renowned orator and trial lawyer, Houston represented the huge Panhandle district in the Texas Senate. When the dilapidated old Texas capitol burned, few tears were shed. (The building was worn out and filthy beyond repair or reclamation. Because of the statehouse, a traveler could smell — before he could see — Austin.)

The state set out to erect a capitol that would command the admiration of the world. At the dedication of that mighty edifice, on May 16, 1888, Houston told the crowd:

> The greatest of states commissions me to say that she accepts this building, and henceforth it shall be the habitation of government. When the title to the noblest edifice upon this hemisphere thus passes from the builder to Texas, reason ordains a brief reference to the deeds and times that eventuate in this occasion .... The architecture of a civilization is its most enduring feature, and by this structure shall Texas transmit herself to posterity ....

—

My favorite Temple Houston story concerns a horse thief who was apprehended while riding the stolen animal. The judge, preparing to hear another case, appointed Houston to defend the thief. He told Houston to take the defendant into the next room and give him "some good advice." The case would be tried later.

When the bailiff was sent to summon the accused, he found Houston sitting beside an open window. The defendant was nowhere in sight. Houston was hailed into court by the angry judge, who demanded to know what had become of the prisoner.

Houston said, "Your honor, you told me to take the accused into that room and give him some good advice. The fact is that with the evidence the state has, the best advice I could give him was that he ought to escape."

—

Greer, Joubert Lee, "The Building of the Texas State Capitol: 1882-1888," M. A. thesis, University of Texas at Austin, 1932.

Roberts, O. M., "The Capitols of Texas," <u>Texas State Historical Association Quarterly</u>, II (October 1898).

# DR. SCOTT SHOT HIS HORSE

Early in this century, Dr. A. C. Scott bought the Gainesville mansion of United States Senator Joseph Weldon Bailey, intending to convert the great house into a hospital. Instead, Scott was hired by the Santa Fe Railroad and he had to move his practice to Temple. (The splendid Bailey home was acquired by the City of Gainesville and remodeled to accommodate Newsome Daugherty Memorial High School — from which I graduated.)

William W. Sterling told of Scott's arrival in Temple. He rapped at the Sterling's door; his hat was crushed, his clothes torn, and his hand was scraped and bleeding. Scott asked Sterling's mother, "Madam, do you have a gun or a pistol in the house?"

Although her husband was away, and she was afraid of firearms, Mrs. Sterling admitted that there was a pistol in the house.

Scott asked to borrow the gun, explaining that he intended to shoot his horse; it had run away and wrecked his buggy. When she wondered if there might be a better way, Scott said,

No ma'am. I could easily trade him off. He is a fine animal. I paid $250 for him only yesterday. I was badly fooled. But I am not going to let some horse trader sell him again and get an innocent person killed. I am not angry, but believe that it is my duty to prevent another runaway.

Dr. Scott led the horse to a hackberry grove, shot him, and returned the gun. Only then did he introduce himself. In this manner a life-long friendship was commenced. Scott considered Mrs. Sterling to be his first patient in Temple.

From his Santa Fe practice grew the Scott and White Clinic — one of the nation's finest medical centers.

—

Sterling, William Warren, <u>Trails and Trials of a Texas Ranger</u>, Norman: University of Oklahoma Press, 1968.

# WILLIAM JACK NEVER FOUGHT A DUEL

Texas had many potential duelists — serious, and not so serious. United States Senator L. T. Wigfall had fled to Marshall after dueling and related altercations ruined his South Carolina law practice.

These so-called affairs of honor were so common that incoming Texas governors — including Mrs. Miriam Amanda Wallace Ferguson —were required to swear that they had fought no duels.

Most duels never came off or were played out at the level of an episode involving Jim Nichols and a ranger we know only as "Dan." In 1841, while on a scout with Jack Hays' rangers, Nichols, having nothing better to do, began arguing with Dan, who finally challenged him.

As recipient of the challenge, Nichols could choose the weapons and dictate the rules of engagement. He selected rifles at a distance of five paces. Standing back-to-back, at a signal Nichols and Dan would walk away, and on the count of three, each would turn and fire.

On the designated morning, the weather was good, and the participants and spectators were excited. Dan's loader, Joe Williams, retired behind some boulders and filled Dan's rifle with a heavy powder charge and some pokeberries. Nichols' loader, John Rodgers, gave his gun a double load of powder and stuffed chunks of pinole down the barrel. (Made from parched cornmeal and brown sugar, pinole was a ranger staple. Rangers on a scout seldom stopped for meals, and pinole dissolved in water helped maintain life until supper — whenever that might be.)

The combatants took position and steps were counted off. They turned and fired. Red pokeberry juice resembling blood covered Nichols' chest. He made a pitiful noise, staggered, and fainted.

Rodgers said, "There, you have kilt Nichols. Look at the blood."

Williams saw the lumps of pinole on Dan's shirt and said, "Dan is kilt, too."

Checking for a wound, Dan touched the warm pinole and passed out.

To their great surprise, Dan and Nichols awoke to find themselves the very best of friends.

—

My favorite dueling story concerns William Jack, a lawyer with very poor eyesight. (Jacksboro and Jack County were named for him and his brother.) Jack habitually made harsh statements, and many Texians wondered how he avoided regular appearances on the field of honor.

In fact, Jack had been challenged to a duel — once. Possessing the right to specify the weapons and terms, the nearly-blind Jack chose shotguns at the width of a dining room table. The challenge was immediately withdrawn, and Jack never received another.

—

# BICKERSTAFF COULD KEEP A SECRET

University of Texas dean T. U. Taylor wrote about a gunman named Bickerstaff who terrorized Alvarado during Reconstruction. He had been a plague upon East Texas before bringing his gang to Johnson County. Bickerstaff would ride into Alvarado,

> ... levy a tribute on the merchants, take what supplies he wanted — money, flour, bacon, feed stuffs — and then go back to his headquarters. This became such a burden that the citizens organized an impromptu vigilante committee which laid plans to end the tribute. Shotguns, rifles, six-shooters were oiled, new caps placed on the tubes loaded with blue whistlers, and every window was provided with a slot out of which the citizens would shoot. Every house around the square was an arsenal ready to fire. Late in the afternoon of April 5, 1869, a lookout gave the word that Bickerstaff was approaching. He saw the merchants closing their doors and others running to cover. He jerked out his six-shooter and yelled, "Rats to your holes."

Taylor, then about ten years old, hiked into Alvarado to share in the excitement. He saw Bickerstaff stop his horse at the hitching rack, throw the reins over a peg, and look about the empty square. He was starting to dismount when the first shot was fired. Bickerstaff and his henchman were blown out of their saddles. Thompson was instantly dead, but Bickerstaff lingered.

A physician who tried to ease Bickerstaff's pain told the

dying man, "You can help this country if you will give us the names of men who have committed certain crimes around here."

The outlaw said, "Doctor, can you keep a secret?"

"Yes, I surely can," the physician answered.

"So can I," said Bickerstaff, as he died.

—

Taylor, T. U., Fifty Years on Forty Acres, Austin: Alec Book Company, 1938.

# DR. WAYLAND FOUNDED A UNIVERSITY IN PLAINVIEW

In 1891, James Henry Wayland, a Louisville School of Medicine graduate, began practicing in Plainview, a Panhandle hamlet consisting of 75 residents, a few meager buildings, and the $10,600, two-story, frame Hale County courthouse.

Dr. Wayland served a huge area. His patients lived below Lubbock, above Amarillo, east of Matador, and well into New Mexico. Plainview's only road was a deeply-rutted trail leading to Amarillo. Wayland navigated the flat, empty country by reference to the sun and stars and a few homes and windmills. (At first, only a single house — near present Tulia — stood between Plainview and Amarillo.) He furnished locust tree seeds for planting around patients' homes to serve as future landmarks in that empty country.

One evening, Wayland left Plainview to treat a patient fifty miles away at the Springlake Ranch. Charting his course by the night sky, he arrived at dawn after having driven across the roof of someone's dugout home. After he got lost and was nearly frozen, Wayland ordered a $5 compass from Montgomery Ward. A local historian wrote:

> In winter he would start out with heated rocks and a heavy wool robe to throw over him in the buggy to break at least a part of the cold .... He carried his gun, a pearl-handled revolver ....

The doctor left carrier pigeons with patients who might need to summon him. Beulah McInnish recalled that, "sometimes a rancher would plow a furrow to his home if it set back too far to be seen easily, and a white sheet over the line usually meant the doctor was needed."

During the World War I influenza epidemic, Wayland's health broke from overwork and exposure, but of his two thousand patients only seven died.

Because of the country's meager educational opportunities, in 1907, Dr. Wayland offered twenty-five acres and $10,000 to found an academy. His gift was conditioned upon the contribution of $40,000 by Baptists and the citizens of Plainview. Eventually, he gave to the project $100,000 — a handsome sum for a man of moderate means who was forced to borrow in order to fulfill his pledges.

Classes began in 1910 at the school that is now Wayland Baptist University.

—

Wofford, Vera, Hale County, Facts and Folklore, Lubbock: Pica Publishing Company, 1978.

# THOMAS TAYLOR SERVED HOWARD PAYNE COLLEGE

Thomas Taylor, who spent most of his life at Brownwood's Howard Payne University, kept that institution alive during the Great Depression.

Born eleven years after Brown County's last Indian raid, Taylor entered the primary grades at Howard Payne, then transferred to Wolf Valley School. After graduation, he returned to Howard Payne — which was then a junior college — and earned his bachelor's degree at Baylor.

Taylor began teaching at Howard Payne College in 1907. As the faculty's bright young man, he was the official driver when the college bought a Model T Ford. Because he was not shown the reverse gear, when Taylor drove a colleague to Sonora, Mexico, they had to get out and push whenever there was a need to back up.

In 1929, as the college faced a disastrous mortgage foreclosure, Taylor became the president of Howard Payne. To keep the college open, he persuaded the faculty to share the tuition income and wait for the balance of their salaries to be paid in better economic times.

The college accepted tuition payments in farm produce, canned goods, and labor. In the end, Taylor persuaded Wichita County philanthropist John G. Hardin and Brownwood businessman J. A. Walker to pay the debts of the college.

---

Dr. Taylor's other contributions included some down-home quotations that deserve to be remembered:

When a pint measure is full, it is not necessary to pour in more.

It is a fine idea to hitch your wagon to a star, but if you expect to get anywhere you had better hitch it to a mule.

It has been well said, because I said it myself.

I will read the scripture lesson from the Third Chapter of Jude. "Business is business," thus saith the Lord.

To a lady professor who fretted about anything, and everything, and nothing, Taylor wrote:

Dear Clara,

It is 14 miles from Whippertown to Boppertown. It is also 14 miles from Boppertown to Whippertown.

Sincerely,

Thomas Taylor.

—

Hinton, William, "A History of Howard Payne College with Emphasis on the Life and Administration of Thomas H. Taylor," Ed. D. dissertation, University of Texas, 1956.

Hitt, Bowling, "History of Howard Payne College," M. A. thesis, Sul Ross State University, 1951.

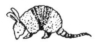

# SOUTHWESTERN COULD NOT BE MOVED FROM GEORGETOWN

Southwestern University was founded, in 1873, to concentrate the educational efforts of Texas Methodists who had divided their support among several tiny colleges. From the first, Southwestern suffered from lack of funds. Local assistance was slight, for only fourteen of five hundred Georgetown residents were Methodists.

Founder Francis Asbury Mood and two others taught thirty-three college students and seventy academy pupils. Worn out by his labors, Mood died at an 1884 conference where he was seeking support for Southwestern.

Women were admitted in 1878 — on a separate campus — and the institution conferred the Mistress of Literature degree. (By 1895, men and women attended classes together.)

In 1898, Dr. R. S. Hyer became the chief executive, and Southwestern's 1906 enrollment exceeded that of any other Methodist institution in the South. But Georgetown was not growing. Many colleges were moving to cities; for instance, Emory University was relocating from Oxford, Georgia, to Atlanta. Texas Christian's president had realized that Waco could not afford both his school and Baylor. Trinity University, at Waxahachie, was shopping for a campus in a major city.

Since the Methodists were about to lose control of Vanderbilt University, they would need a strong institution in a major city. Hyer began investigating the removal of Southwestern from Georgetown.

When Southwestern opened, the University of Texas had not been established, and Baylor was located in Independence, but by 1900 the state university, in Austin, was prospering, and the Baptist university was flourishing at Waco.

Both Dallas and Fort Worth were interested in hosting Southwestern, but resistance among alumni, students, and Methodists, resulted in an injunction to retain Southwestern in Georgetown. Hyer resigned his position and was the founding president of Texas Wesleyan University, which soon became Southern Methodist University. W. W. Caruth's offer of land adjoining the proposed 300-acre Highland Park tract settled the matter of location.

Hyer's last official duty at Southwestern was conferring degrees upon a class that included J. Frank Dobie. New president Charles Bishop told the graduates:

> It is true that our neighbor, Dallas, wanted to take Southwestern, and surely she needs it. It is true that Fort Worth fought to get Southwestern, and surely she needs the influence of such an institution more than she needs anything else; but it is true also that Southwestern University is still at Georgetown; that she will be here through the centuries to come.

—

Brown, Ray Hyer, Robert Stewart Hyer. The Man I Knew, Salado: Anson Jones Press, 1957.

Thomas, Mary Martha, Southern Methodist University, Dallas: Southern Methodist University Press, 1974.

# ROBERT HYER FOUNDED SOUTHERN METHODIST UNIVERSITY

President Robert Hyer, of Southwestern University, was a brilliant physicist whose pioneering work in radio was hampered by the demands of running a college. He may have built the first X-ray machine.

Georgetown had two telephone companies — one for local calls. To talk to someone in another town, a patron placed his call at the long distance company office. After six o'clock in the evening, service was available at the county jail.

Remembering her father's trips downtown to receive long distance calls — usually late at night — Ray Hyer Brown wrote:

> He would dress and walk down to the jail to have some doting mother ask how her boy was. Most likely he was either a prep student or a freshman and father didn't even know him. After several such trips, father gave instructions at the jail to receive no more night calls for him. Following one of these night trips his discourse at chapel the next morning would be on the subject of writing home to your parents at least once a week.

Hyer was reluctant to employ anyone who moved slowly, his daughter recalled, he believed any man worth his salt carried a good pocket knife, and he was convinced that any adult could wrap a package neatly.

During the campaign to raise funds for the new Southern Methodist University, an important dinner was hosted by a

Dallas banker. The party included several wealthy men and some Methodist ministers. The dessert was watermelon and, with the first bite, Dr. Hyer realized that something had been added. The cook had laced the melon liberally with hard liquor. Hyer reported that the preachers thoroughly enjoyed that dessert. In fact, two of them picked up watermelon seeds and slipped them into their pockets.

—

Brown, Ray Hyer, <u>Robert Stewart Hyer, The Man I Knew</u>, Salado: Anson Jones Press, 1957.

# CARLTON COLLEGE HELPED SHAPE BONHAM

Charles Carlton, born in Kent County, England, ran away to sea at age sixteen. In Virginia, he studied under Alexander Campbell, and he graduated from Bethany College in 1849.

When turmoil attending the secession controversy disrupted his teaching in Springfield, Missouri, Carlton moved to Texas. (He organized the Dallas congregation that became Central Christian Church.) Hoping to return home after the war, Carlton sojourned in Grayson County. Randolph Clark wrote:

> At the close of the war, while waiting for peace to be restored in Missouri, he secured a building in the village of Kentuckytown and began teaching. The school was crowded from the first day. Many had been deprived of the opportunities of going to school through the years of war, and lost no time in taking advantage of this privilege. After the second year, he decided to remain in Texas. The citizens of Bonham offered him a suitable building and equipment and he moved and settled permanently in their midst.

Clark declared that nothing resembling Carlton's school existed later.

> The teacher was the school; students came from far and near, many of them boys in years, who had developed into men by the hardships of war. The school was to them the opportunity for making up for the four years which had been cut out of their lives when they would have been getting an education.

Clark and his brother, Addison, were both Confederate veterans. As Charles Carlton had gone out into the world emulating his mentor, Alexander Campbell, the Clarks followed Carlton's example. In the process they founded the institution that became Texas Christian University.

—

Clark, Randolph, <u>Reminiscences</u>, Fort Worth: Texas Christian University Press, 1979.

Hay, Kenneth, <u>Life and Influence of Charles Carlton</u>, Fort Worth: 1940.

Taylor, T. U., <u>Fifty Years on Forty Acres</u>, Austin: Alec Book Company, 1938.

# CHARLES CARLTON IMPOSED A UNIQUE PUNISHMENT

For thirty-four years, Carlton College served Bonham, where founder Charles Carlton also organized the Christian Church. University of Texas dean T. U. Taylor wrote:

> Since the news of Uncle Charlie Carlton's school methods and training methods had spread all over North Texas ... I ... entered Carlton Seminary in the fall of 1877, and there I met one of those rare and radiant characters who used money as axle grease and was ever building character in the minds of the pupils, boys and girls... Charles Carlton was a young boy in the shipyards of Boston working as a day laborer. One day he spelled out in the newspaper the word "algebra." He told me that at the time he did not know whether it was a snake or an elephant, but he asked his boss what the word spelled and the boss replied, "You ought to go to Alexander Campbell."

> No poor boy ever went to Charlie Carlton, broke and helpless, and was turned away from his door.... As a teacher he had few equals and no superior.

> Charles Carlton taught from 8 a. m. to 6 p. m. and each weekend, after teaching Sunday School for two hours, he preached a sermon in the Bonham Church.

A Bonham writer believed that

> ... the outstanding event of importance to this town was the coming of Uncle Charley Carlton to establish the school and later organize a congregation and form a

church here. Bonham, then a small village, grew up around Carlton College.

Carlton sat on the stage at one end of a big upstairs room, and pupils moved to the bench in front of him to recite. Taylor stated:

> He never taught two classes the same way and never let a student, however old, get out of English grammar. He would ask a special student if he understood a special problem. If the student said, "Yes," then came back the demand, "Stand up and tell us what you understand".... Woe be unto the boy or girl who would tell him that he "understood" it and then failed in the job of explaining it. He ruled that school with a rod of love. In two years I never saw him whip a boy, but I have seen many boys beg him to whip them.

Carlton's method of punishment was unique. Summoning an offender to the dais, he would seat the boy on his lap and ask if he wanted his parents informed about his misbehavior. By then everyone was watching, and the culprit was weeping. Citing his duty to punish him severely, Carlton would kiss the boy on the cheek. The pupils would collapse in laughter, while the offender returned to his seat, knowing that his humiliation would be known all over Fannin County. There were few repeaters.

—

Hay, Kenneth, <u>Life and Influence of Charles Carlton</u>, Fort Worth: 1940.

Taylor, T. U., <u>Fifty Years on Forty Acres</u>, Austin: Alec Book Company, 1938.

# THE CLARKS ESTABLISHED ADDRAN MALE AND FEMALE COLLEGE

In 1854, John Peter Smith, a graduate of Alexander Campbell's Bethany College, opened Fort Worth's first school. During Reconstruction, Smith was teaching again, but he preferred to practice law.

In 1869, Smith persuaded Addison Clark to take charge of the school, which occupied the Masonic Hall's ground floor. Clark's brother, Randolph, was teaching in Birdville. That fall, the Clarks opened the Male and Female Seminary of Fort Worth in a small, frame building owned by the First Christian Church. Addison, Randolph, and their father, Joseph Addison Clark, preached there. (The Disciples of Christ had paid $200 for the block bounded by 4th, 5th, Main and Houston streets and were constructing a church of brick.)

Addison, born in Morris County, on December 11, 1842, and Randolph, who was born in Harrison County in 1844, were Confederate veterans. The Clarks sought to follow in the footsteps of their mentor, Charles Carlton, whose photograph occupied a place of honor in their school. (Addison Clark married Carlton's niece.)

Fort Worth was a rowdy place—headquarters for "the tough vagabond and the professional gambler." Randolph Clark recalled that,

> ... in 1873 the village became suddenly disturbed, really hysterically excited over the railroad and the prospect of a city right at once. This made it not a

desirable place to assemble young people for training.

The situation caused the Clarks to purchase the two-story, stone schoolhouse Pleasant Thorp had erected in Hood County. Thorp Spring had daily stage service to Weatherford. Randolph and his father opened the Thorp Spring school in September of 1873 while Addison fulfilled obligations to his Fort Worth pupils.

AddRan Male and Female College — named for Addison's deceased son, AddRan — opened with thirteen pupils, but by June the enrollment was 123. Although it was affiliated with the Disciples of Christ, the Thorp Spring school was a family operation. Addison was president, Randolph, vice president, their father, Joseph, was treasurer, and a brother, Thomas, taught languages and music.

The school's catalog declared that students would have "neither the time nor the desire for miscellaneous gallantry or letter writing" and would "never dream of matrimony until their education is finished."

—

Clark, Randolph, Reminiscences, Fort Worth: Texas Christian University Press, 1979.

Hay, Kenneth, Life and Influence of Charles Carlton, Fort Worth: 1940.

Moore, Jerome, Texas Christian University: A Hundred Years of History, Fort Worth: Texas Christian University Press, 1974.

# ADDRAN BECAME TEXAS CHRISTIAN UNIVERSITY

Tuition for the AddRan Male and Female College primary department was $2 a month in 1873. College students paid $5. Board cost $12 a month. The rules forbade liquor, tobacco, profanity and the possession of guns and Bowie knives.

Uniforms were required. Women wore bonnets and grey woolen dresses with checked gingham aprons; black dresses, white aprons, and hats were prescribed for Sundays. Men wore "Gray Janes, or Cassimere and black hats."

The first degrees were granted in 1876. Enrollment reached 201, but a depression forced the Clarks into default on the purchase note they had given for the Thorp Spring campus. Pleasant Thorp foreclosed, and Randolph Clark sold his Fort Worth home and his wife's property to buy a new campus at Thorp Spring.

The Clarks invested everything in the college — their time and meager savings. Randolph stated that "Addison worked for almost nothing. One session the janitor received more money than was paid the president."

Without an endowment the school eventually would fail, so, in 1889, the Clarks donated AddRan College to the Disciples of Christ, a move they believed to be "the surest and quickest way to get the college endowed and firmly established."

A new charter changed the name to AddRan Christian University. Addison Clark remained president, and Charles Carlton, of Bonham, was a trustee.

In February of 1894 occurred an important event involving

the use of instrumental music in a student revival. The college organ had never been played in Sunday worship services attended by people from the town.

The chapel was packed on that Sunday, and most of those present held strong convictions on the subject of instrumental music. The organist, Bertha Mason Fuller, told Dr. Colby Hall that as the service began, Joseph Addison Clark walked down the aisle to the rostrum, where Addison stood at the pulpit, and

> Feeling in his pocket, he took out a folded paper and reached up to Brother Addison who leaned down to take it. (I can see the scene now as clearly as then; the face of the aged saint appealing to his eldest son.)

After conferring with Randolph, Addison Clark announced that although he was inclined to grant the petition forbidding use of the organ, he had given permission to the students, and he could not break his word.

> His voice was soft and gentle.... He bowed his head and stood silent for a few moments, then turning toward Bro. Douthitt, who was still standing by the organ, baton in hand, he lifted his right hand saying, "Play on Miss Bertha."

About 140 people walked out, led by Joseph Addison Clark, with tears streaming down his cheeks and "his cane punctuating the hymn." AddRan professor Charles W. Howard told Dr. Hall that:

> ... some wanted to work over the organ with an axe and throw it in the creek.... Next morning Mr. Randolph said to me: "It will ruin us. Those old brethren in the country won't let us preach in their schoolhouses." And it did. They only lasted one more year and the school, having fallen off, moved to Waco....

Many believed the incident precipitated the school's removal from Thorp Spring. (Controversy in the brotherhood during that time resulted in formation of the Church of Christ and the Christian Church.)

AddRan Christian University opened on January 2, 1896 at the campus of the defunct Waco Female College. Baylor president Rufus Burleson helped welcome AddRan to McLennan County.

Randolph wrote that Addison Clark

... preferred they would take the school and leave him, but he was the school and must go. Few ever knew what it cost him. He said to me, "I would rather work here the rest of my life, die and be buried in these hills, than go anywhere, or have anything, any city can give."

Randolph returned to Thorp Spring, where he conducted Jarvis Institute, a preparatory school and junior college. In 1899, Addison resigned as president of AddRan Christian University.

Renamed Texas Christian University, the college still had financial problems. After the main building burned, on March 23, 1910, the trustees voted to move to a large city.

Fort Worth, Gainesville, McKinney, and Dallas wanted T. C. U. The situation was complicated by competition for the new Methodist university, which was finally won by Dallas.

As construction on the present campus proceeded, classes in school year 1910-1911 were held downtown, across from the Tarrant County courthouse.

Addison Clark died in Comanche at his daughter's home on May 13, 1911, as the college founded by his family completed its first year in Fort Worth. Randolph Clark died in 1935.

Professor Howard recalled that in the school's early days:

We had many fine young people, and many who should have been in jail, and were later. Mr. Addison

whaled the life half out of some of those 18 and 20 year
old fellows with a limb for stealing chickens, fighting,
and shooting craps. He was a disciplinarian of the old
school. He had no confidence in the bad ones but could
be imposed on by the young preachers to any limit, if
they made a long, sanctimonious face, even by those
who secretly went to Fort Worth to gamble and roll
'em high, if they kept him deceived.

—

Clark, Randolph, Reminiscences, Fort Worth: Texas Christian University Press,
1979.

Hall, Colby, Texas Disciples, Fort Worth: Texas Christian University Press, 1953.

Moore, Jerome, Texas Christian University: A Hundred Years of History, Fort
Worth: Texas Christian University Press, 1974.

# BORDEN COUNTY'S LAND RUSHES WERE UNIQUE

Borden County, the site of the most unusual land rushes ever seen in the West, was created in 1876, as the legislature — using ruler and pencil to establish lines some thirty miles apart — converted a vast territory into 55 counties.

The county and the seat were named for Gail Borden, the inventor of condensed milk and founder of the Borden Company. Gail had the only post office between Big Spring and Lubbock.

In 1880, Borden County had thirty-five residents; a decade later, the population was 222, and the county was organized in 1891. The deed records were brought from Big Spring, and two men built a $477 courthouse that was used mainly for dances. A watermelon patch covered the square.

The land rushes grew out of the state's decision to sell local school lands. The first person to make application on sale day had his choice of available parcels. Farmers wanted the land as much as the cattlemen, who sent cowhands to buy the tracts. The price was $1 an acre, payable 1/40th down and the balance over forty years at 3% interest.

On sale day, cowboys and farmers fought to be at the head of the line when the clerk opened for business. Cattlemen wore blue ribbons and nesters red; both sides were wise enough to leave their weapons at home. Arthur Prince saw,

> ... a large band of horsemen coming into town at a hard run. They dismount and converge on the courthouse where they immediately begin the process of dragging out another bunch of men who are already there. They just grab the other men and rastle and scuffle and drag

them out. No gun play. The cowboys have dragged the nesters out of the courthouse and they will stay there until a few days later the settlers have obtained reinforcements and are now able to drag the cowboys out, which they proceed to do.

Farmers obtaining land could not always remain. Meager rainfall accomplished what cowboys had not been able to achieve when courthouse scuffles determined how much of the county would be farmland.

The Borden Sun once carried this masthead statement:

Published every Thursday out in West Texas... where they raise 2,000 pound steers, fine sheep, where the antelope roams and the coyote howls, where everybody is friendly and life is worth living. Borden County, where a bale of cotton an acre has been grown, is on State Highway 15 on the way to Carlsbad Caverns. Nobody on WPA, nobody on relief, a healthy climate and not a single doctor in Borden County.

—

Kraeger, Peter H. "A History of the Early Days of Borden County or How Gail Borden Found Immortality," 1972.

The Borden Citizen, September 1969.

# HARVEY MITCHELL WAS THE NAVASOTA COUNTY GOVERNMENT

Boonville, the Navasota County capital, was an interesting place in the 1850s. (Navasota became Brazos County, and Bryan succeeded Boonville as the seat of government.) Because only forty-five families — about 150 people — lived in the county, little work was required of officials, and their compensation was practically nothing. Since no one could afford to serve, a man would accept election only if he did not have to perform the duties of his office. The solution was for someone to assume the responsibilities of all the officials.

Two families lived in Boonville, and Harvey Mitchell held all the county offices when a couple bound for Milam County stopped at Mitchell's store and post office. Their horse had thrown a shoe, and Mitchell corrected that problem in his blacksmith shop. County Clerk Mitchell issued a marriage license and, as chief justice, married them. When the groom asked if there was anything he did not do, Mitchell said that he was the district clerk, sheriff, tax assessor and collector, road overseer, and surveyor. He farmed, ran the mill, and was the only steward of the Methodist church.

Boonville's jail was a log dungeon. A trap door in the roof permited ingress and egress by a ladder that could be lowered inside. An unfortunate from another county had been incarcerated for weeks when a storm occurred one evening. Next morning, the locks were broken, the ladder was down in the hole, and the prisoner was gone.

At the next term of court, the prisoner appeared and begged

for bail, or trial — or just to be hanged. Billions of fleas had rendered the jail unendurable. Even after his acquittal — when there was no possibility of any negative consequences — the prisoner's explanation of his escape remained that lightning broke the locks, opened the trap door, and dropped the ladder down inside the cell.

—

Marshall, Elmer Grady, "The History of Brazos County, Texas," M. A. thesis, University of Texas, 1937.

Wilcox, Lois, "The Early History of Bryan," M. A. thesis, University of Texas at Austin, 1952.

# HORSES HELPED ORGANIZE CASTRO COUNTY

Plains counties had a tough time starting to do business, for the law required the signatures of at least 150 voters in order to organize.

Created in 1876, Castro County had only nine residents in the 1890 federal census. They were probably the family and cowhands of James Carter, the owner of the 7-Up Ranch.

After every citizen had signed, the petition still lacked names. Travelers were solicited, and the signatures of relatives who had never visited the Plains were forged. Finally, Carter's horses were given surnames and added to the instrument — Bill, Jim, Tom, Joe, Sam and other Carters.

The Oldham County commissioners, who supervised the infant county, honored the petition, and Castro was organized in 1891.

Lumber was hauled from Amarillo for the two-story, $12,000, frame courthouse. The unpartitioned upstairs was ideal for dancing. The cupola offered the best breeze in the county. A ladder nailed to the side of the building gave cowboys access to the poker game that was always in progress on top of the Castro capitol.

Because of the flimsy jail and the likelihood of escape, an early sheriff would take a really bad prisoner home and sleep handcuffed to him.

After fire leveled the courthouse in 1906, materials for a new building were brought from Hereford by a freighter who hitched five wagons to a steam engine and crossed the country in the manner of a trackless railroad.

One morning, during a labor dispute, he discovered that the nuts which held in place the steam engine's wheels were missing. After the freighter surrendered to the employees' demands — as if by magic — a tow sack containing the wheel nuts was discovered in a nearby creek.

—

Castro County Diamond Jubilee, Inc., <u>History of the First Seventy-Five Years of Castro County, Texas</u>, Dimmitt: 1966.

# MCKINNEY HAD THE TALLEST BUILDING NORTH OF SAN ANTONIO

When McKinney was made the Collin County seat, in 1848, the first courthouse was a log cabin. Because of disagreements over responsibility for building and tending the fire, a new two-room, frame courthouse was soon built of lumber hauled from Jefferson.

At Christmas, pits were dug for a two-day barbeque. Beef, deer, and wild turkey dinners were served to all comers, and a great tent was erected on the square for dancing. But that soiree did not measure up to the 1876 New Years Day party celebrating completion of the new Collin County temple of justice — the tallest building north of San Antonio.

Downstairs, tables borrowed from hotels were covered with unbleached domestic, and coal oil lamps and Chinese lanterns hung from the ceilings. In the second floor district courtroom, Rudolph's Silver Cornet Band performed.

Several days of heavy rainfall in McKinney jeopardized the party's success. Mud was shoetop-deep on the square, and downtown streets could not be traversed by wagon or carriage unless they were pulled by double teams.

Sheriff Bill Merritt and a couple of dozen other men waded ankle-deep water and mud to lay planks across fence posts so guests could attend the ball.

Inside the courthouse, elegantly-dressed ladies and gentlemen of Collin and neighboring counties danced to "The Blue Danube Waltz."

At midnight, a thousand Texans trooped downstairs to supper, which was consumed standing, for chairs were in short supply. Dancing continued until three o'clock in the morning.

—

Hall, Helen and Hall, Roy, <u>Collin County</u>, Quanah:  Nortex Press, 1975.

# THE COURTHOUSE WAS THE CENTER OF ALL THE WORLD THAT MATTERED

In old Texas, the courthouse was the most important building in a county seat town. There the great men met to levy taxes, try law suits, and campaign for office. There the records of deeds and marriages and births and deaths were maintained. Candidates for governor, attorney general, senator, congressman, and sheriff spoke from the courthouse steps. And there, beneath the great oaks, aged philosophers in faded workshirts and overalls convened to chew tobacco, inspect passersby, trade pocket knives and — as William Saroyan would have put it — pass the time of life.

The courthouse was dear to small-town Texans. The tower clock provided a standard time for the community; one of the four faces could be seen from any point. Anyone wishing to know the hour simply stepped out his front door and looked toward the square. Of course, there was a possibility of error. The timepiece on top of the old Comanche County temple of justice had a poor reputation; some citizens claimed that no two of the clock's faces had ever agreed.

The great bell in the tower of Red River County's old castle began tolling at 2:30 o'clock one morning and clanged four hundred times before the janitor restored quiet. My old friend Weldon Hart claimed that it was later in Clarksville that morning than ever before or since.

The people of the Plains may have loved their courthouses more than other Texans, perhaps because they made greater personal use of them. The Donley County capitol's top floor was used for dancing because of a chronic shortage of jurors. A dance was a sure-fire method of luring cowboys into Clarendon. Many trial delays were avoided by the judge's ability to send the sheriff upstairs to collar dancing cowboys for service on underpopulated juries.

Tax-supported frivolity did not please everyone. In Carson County, the floor had to be replaced every other year because the dancers wore it out. Some taxpayers were incensed over paying for such wear and tear when they seldom — or never — danced.

The courthouses accommodated the first schools, church services, and meetings of all kinds; however, the highest and best use of the building was as the site of the community Christmas tree. In the Plains country, where people were begining to get a toehold, where money was hard to come by — and trees even more scarce — an under-nourished cedar would be hauled in from the Canadian River breaks. The base would be nailed to the floor and the top wired to the ceiling. Everyone would help decorate the tree with strings of popcorn and homemade paper ornaments.

On Christmas Eve, farmers, ranchers, and cowhands from thirty miles around would gather for an annual visit, to watch the children open presents, and to experience the emotion Paul Crume called "that quiet singing in the heart that is Christmas."

—

Crume, Paul, The Dallas Morning News, December 25, 1958.

# SAM BASS' BUDDY BURNED DENTON'S COURTHOUSE

In 1856, the Denton County seat was moved to a hundred-acre site in the present city of Denton, where wild turkeys and prairie chickens were plentiful.

A two-story capitol was built north of the square because,

Sand was so deep on the courthouse square that there was danger of wagons and buggies "sticking," and the weeds on the public square grew to be as tall as a man's head. Cattle from the range wandered unmolested through the city's so-called streets.

When that courthouse burned in 1875, most public records were destroyed. Evidence showed that someone had tried to destroy pending indictments against Sam Bass.

The Cumberland Presbyterian Church was designated as the temporary seat of justice. When that church caught fire, earlier suspicions were fed, and Sam Bass' friend, Henry Underwood, was indicted and jailed.

The $40,000 courthouse which was completed in 1877 may have been Denton's first brick building. When lightning rendered the courthouse unsafe, in 1894, it was demolished.

The present temple of justice, designed by W. C. Dodson, was completed in 1896. To preserve an oak tree whose branches had shaded soldiers as they were mustered into Confederate service, the courthouse was not placed in the center of the square.

Legend teaches that the first time Sam Bass saw the Denton Mare — the beast whose ownership caused the racing losses that turned Bass toward a life of crime — she was tethered to that oak.

All that remains of that celebrated tree is an empty circle in the sidewalk where it stood.

—

Anon, <u>Life and Adventures of Sam Bass, the Notorious Union Pacific and Texas Train Robber</u>, Dallas: Dallas Commercial Steam Printing , 1878.

Bridges, C. A., <u>A History of Denton County, Texas</u>, 1978. The <u>Denton Record-Chronicle</u>, January 31, 1971.

# PANCHO VILLA THREW JIM HOGG COUNTY INTO A PANIC

Jim Hogg County, which was named for the first native-born Texas governor, was created and organized in 1913.

A few years earlier, longhorns grazed the area in such great numbers that they were not worth driving to market. They were killed by the tens of thousands for their hides, and a later "bone boom" was precipitated, as horns and skeletons were gathered and hauled to Laredo for shipment to England, where they were made into buttons and knife handles.

A native of Denmark, Viggo Kohler, gave the land for the public square in Hebbronville, the town that grew up beside the railroad tracks.

At first, only about thirty men were eligible to serve on juries, and they were called frequently. A Jim Hogg County grand juror at one session could expect to be summoned for petit jury service at the next term of court.

A rancher on jury duty would bring his family for a sojourn of a few days at the Viggo Hotel. It was a welcome opportunity for women to enjoy meals prepared by someone else and to visit with neighbors whose husbands were also in Hebbronville as jurors.

The county was regularly thrown into turmoil by rumors of raids by Pancho Villa's banditos. Families would flee their ranches and take refuge in Hebbronville.

Once, Roscoe Roper—costumed as Pancho Villa—galloped his horse into the crowd at the Fiesta on the Plaza, firing his pistols into the air. The Plaza emptied quickly, and the surprised and dispirited Roper was arrested by Sheriff Oscar Thompson. He was fined $17.50 for the prank.

—

Hebronville Chamber of Commerce, <u>Fiftieth Anniversary, Jim Hogg County</u>, Hebronville: 1963

# COWBOYS LEVELED GRAYSON'S COURTHOUSE TO SETTLE A BET

When Grayson County was organized, in 1846, the population was about 500. Completion of a $232 courthouse occasioned a celebration that included a barrel of whiskey, barbecue, and two fiddlers.

Because water and wood were scarce at the original site, Sherman was relocated, and the courthouse was sold. To clear a road to the present square, T. J. Shannon used six yoke of oxen to drag a tree trunk through the brush and briars.

A pecan tree on the courthouse square functioned as the seat of justice in 1848; cases were tried in its shade. The tree also fulfilled other community needs. On Sundays, preachers conducted services beneath the branches, while worshippers kept their rifles handy in case of Indian attack. Weekdays, the tree was a post office. Letters were posted in the pockets of an old coat that hung from a limb for transport by travelers, and incoming mail was left there to be claimed by addressees. The tree had banking functions also; by unspoken common consent, property parked there was not to be molested. Saddlebags containing valuables were thrown across a branch while the owners attended to business in Sherman. The pecan tree bank was never robbed.

In 1858, a courthouse was torn down to settle a bet two cowhands had made on whether a gray goose was nesting beneath the floor. Because legal instruments had to be posted at the courthouse entrance, the Grayson County sheriff was forced to dig out the door from under the wreckage and lean it against a tree in order to nail up foreclosure notices.

The first brick courthouse, built in 1859, was utilized for dancing, preaching, and theatricals. After a year of heavy wear, the commissioners ordered three inches of sawdust laid down to protect such floor as had not been used up.

First Monday was Trade Day, or Stray Sale Day. Once, a stranger came into Sherman on a small pony, without a cent to his name, and after trading horses all day he departed on his original mount with $20 in his pocket.

A lynch mob burned Grayson's courthouse on May 9, 1930, and the present temple of justice — the county's fifth — was dedicated in 1935.

—

Landrum, Graham and Smith, Allan, Grayson County, Fort Worth: Historical Publishers, 1967.

Lucas, Mattie and Hall, Mita, A History of Grayson County, Sherman: Scruggs Printing Company, 1936.

# YOUNG COUNTY WAS CLOSED FOR BUSINESS

General David Twiggs' surrender of United States military installations to Texas Confederates, in 1861, had serious consequences for residents of the frontier. Aware that the troops were gone and the whites were fighting among themselves, Indians attacked the settlers. As Governor Sam Houston put it, the frontier was bleeding from every pore.

Young was one of the counties depopulated by the Indian menace during the Civil War. The seat of government was Belknap, a hamlet that had sprung up beside Fort Belknap. Always subject to heavy depredations, the area was more exposed than ever before to Indian attack.

Although the 1860 population was 500 whites and 92 slaves, after secession just three families — Williams, Johnson, and George — remained in the Fort Belknap neighborhood.

Only a handful held on elsewhere in Young County. (After the war — at a time when federal troops had occupied Texas nearly five years — the total population in the 1870 census consisted of only 135 whites and 4 blacks.)

As settlers retreated to safety in the eastern counties, finally Young did not have enough men to maintain the government. The last officials delivered the county's record books to the Jack County judge, at Jacksboro, for safekeeping pending a time when it might again be possible for civilization to return.

Later, a soldier at Fort Belknap wrote, "Quite a village had existed here before the war, but at the time of our arrival only a few families lived in the entire county, and primeval solitude reigned."

Upon the reorganization of Young County, in 1874, the new town of Graham was made the seat of government. There, beneath a huge live oak tree, forty cattlemen formed the first effective organization against rustling, the Texas and Southwestern Cattle Raisers Association.

—

Johnson, Carrie, A History of Young County, Texas, Austin: Texas State Historical Association, 1956.

McConnell, H. H., Five Years A Cavalryman, Jacksboro: J. N. Rogers & Company, 1889.

Young County Historical Survey Committee, Graham Centennial History: 1872-1972, 1972.

# WOODY STORIES ABOUND IN WISE COUNTY

In a fine Wise County history, G. Q. Woody recalled his father's participation in an Indian fight near Olney. The twelve settlers included Dick, a black man. The battle had gone on several hours when Dick told Woody, "If we don't get that chief they are going to keep us here all night."

Woody shot the chief, and the Indians carried him away. But fearing that the enemy's retreat was a trick, the settlers remained under cover until dawn. G. Q. Woody said,

> Old man Kooch, who lived in Jacksboro for several years and died not too many years ago, had an arrow stuck in his leg, and every time he would move, his pants leg would move that arrow and it would hurt like "thunder." My daddy said he bet they turned him over 100 times that night, but didn't ever think about pulling it out, you know. So they got a doctor the next morning and the first thing he did was pull that arrow out, and he was alright then.

On their way home from the army, Sam Woody and C. C. Leonard were walking along a railroad track near Dallas on a very dark night. While crossing a trestle, they realized that a train was coming. Unable to see the ground, they could not know how much of a fall they would have should they be knocked off — or have to jump from — the track. Dropping down beside the trestle, they

... hung onto the crossties until the train was gone, and

then they were so weak they couldn't get back up. Uncle Sam said he told Mr. Leonard to pray a while and then he would, and said when they got so tired they couldn't hold on any longer they let go and they were within about a foot of the ground.

G. Q. Woody recalled that,

Uncle Sam used to tell this and just die laughing. It was at night, you see, and they didn't know how far they were from the ground. Mr. Leonard would just sit there and grin.

—

Wise County Historical Commission, <u>Wise County History</u>, Volume II, Decatur: 1982.

# NOCONA BOOTS STAGED A PONY EXPRESS RACE

In 1939, the Great Depression was still the main fact of economic life in the United States. The Texas Centennial had stimulated activity in 1936, and now both New York and San Francisco were staging world fairs.

In a less ambitious effort to make something happen, Enid Justin's Nocona Boot Company sponsored a modern pony express run. The winner of the two thousand-mile race from Nocona, Texas to the San Francisco Fair would receive 750 new silver dollars.

On March 1, 1939, five thousand spectators saw seventeen men — and one woman — gallop out of Nocona, bound for California. Each contestant had two horses. At stations situated twenty-five miles apart, an assistant would saddle the rested animal, load the tired mount into a trailer, and drive to the next stop. Judges decided how many times a horse might be ridden each day.

Several contestants soon dropped out, leaving a dozen serious cowboys. The only non-Texan — T. J. Sykes, of Debo, Oklahoma — held the lead until one of his horses gave out near El Paso. Eight men finished the race.

George Cates, a favorite of the spectators, would regularly dismount and run a mile in order to spare his mounts. Near Los Angeles one of his horses foundered, but the judges allowed Cates to continue with a single animal, on the understanding that, if necessary, the original pony express riders completed their missions on foot. Running alternate stretches of twenty-five miles, Cates finished in third place.

In Ventura, California, Chris Uselton was in the process of taking the lead when a car struck him and his horse, and he was forced to withdraw.

The winner was Shannon Davidson, of Matador, who crossed the finish line in downtown Oakland at 2 o'clock p. m. on March 24. His mounts — Ranger and Rocket — had carried him 2,018 miles in just over twenty-three days.

—

Ferguson, Henry N., "Enid Justin, Woman Bootmaker," <u>Texas Woman</u>, February 1979.

# REYNOLDS CARRIED A COMANCHE ARROWHEAD IN HIS BACK

In April of 1867, George Reynolds and nine others pursued a Comanche war party into present Haskell County and caught up with them near the Double Mountain Fork of the Brazos River.

In the ensuing battle, Reynolds was shot. The arrow was deflected by the United States Army belt buckle he was wearing and entered just above the navel. He pulled out the arrow, but the head came off the shaft. (Plains Indians sometimes designed their arrows so the point would remain; should the victim not be killed immediately, infection caused by the arrowhead might still claim him.)

Reynolds' sister wrote that, to get the wounded man home,

> They tied two horses together, heads and tails, and filled in between with their packs.... These were placed across the horses and filled in with bedding, and the wounded man was laid on this improvised bed. A man on each side led the horses as the slow journey home was begun.

In this fashion, Reynolds was taken sixty painful miles to the Old Stone Ranch, where his father had settled the year before.

Since no physician would gamble upon trying to extract the arrowhead, Reynolds lived in pain for fifteen years. Finally, in Kansas City, Missouri, Dr. W. M. Lewis agreed to attempt the surgery.

At the St. James Hotel — in the absence of hospitals, out-of-town patients were treated at hotels — Lewis and two other physicians removed the arrowhead, which Reynolds kept as a souvenir, along with the surgeon's certificate that he had "successfully removed a 'steel' or 'iron' arrowhead from the back of George T. Reynolds, of Fort Griffin, Texas... [which had] entered his body in front and passed directly through his abdominal cavity and lodged in the muscles of his back."

Sallie Reynolds Matthews said that no anesthesia was used. During the surgery, Abel Head "Shanghai" Pierce and another friend remained with Reynolds, who had made the surgeon promise that he would halt the operation if told to do so.

Pierce became excited and shouted, "Stop, doctor, you are cutting that man to the hollow." Mrs. Matthews wrote,

> At this my brother called a halt. The cut had missed the arrowhead, and had gone down by the side of it. Brother raised himself to a sitting posture and bent forward. The steel arrow head slipped out into the incision.

—

Evans, Joe M., Bloys Cowboy Camp Meeting, El Paso: Guynes Printing Company, 1959.

Matthews, Sallie Reynolds, Interwoven, Austin: University of Texas Press, 1958.

# THE ROPE WALKER DIED ON A CORSICANA STREET

Near the end of the nineteenth century, a 69-year-old, one-legged, tightwire walker contracted to perform in downtown Corsicana. (His peg leg was fitted with a deep groove to accommodate a rope.)

As a promotion calculated to attract shoppers to the business section, the performer would walk a rope stretched across Corsicana's main thoroughfare and anchored to the roofs of business buildings on either side of Beaton Street. Whether the idea belonged to him or was suggested by the merchants, the performer would walk the rope with a cast iron cook stove strapped onto his back.

On July 28, 1898, Corsicana was crowded with spectators. As the rope walker eased away from a building, the stove's weight made the rope sag more than he had anticipated. Halfway across Beaton Street, the performer fell to the pavement, mortally injured.

A physician asked whether the rope walker wanted a minister, but there was no answer. Then Abe Mulkey, a young Methodist preacher who would build a national reputation as an evangelist, asked how he might help the injured man. He whispered, "Please get a rabbi. I am Jewish."

Since Corsicana had no rabbi, a Jewish merchant prayed with the dying man. The performer had told witnesses that he was born February 6, 1829 in Princeton, New Jersey, but if he ever spoke his name, no one remembered — or reported — it. (Apparently there had been no written contract.)

For years, efforts were made to determine the performer's identity , without success, and he rests in Corsicana's Hebrew Cemetery beneath a stone inscribed with two words: "Rope Walker."

—

Corsicana Daily Sun, June 29, 1976.

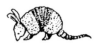

# JUDGE BAYLOR DEVISED A SOBRIETY TEST

---

Several times the United States disappointed Texians in the matter of annexation. When joinder to the old states finally was effected, the time was right for serious celebration.

Noah Smithwick was in Bastrop when news came that President James K. Polk had approved the annexation legislation. Judge Robert Emmett Bledsoe Baylor, an ordained Baptist minister and a founder of Baylor University, was then holding court in Bastrop. (Baylor preached in the evenings and on Sundays when he was traveling the circuit.)

Baylor announced the "glad tidings" of annexation to those in the courtroom and quoted with approval the ruling of Chief Justice John Marshall that, "No man should be considered drunk on Independence Day, so long as he could pronounce the word 'Epsom.'"

Convinced that Marshall's rule should govern the observance of that important event, as Texas passed from republic to one of the United States, Judge Baylor "therefore adjourned the court till 10 o'clock the next morning that we might celebrate, and celebrate we did with a will." Smithwick recalled that,

> In the absence of cannon we brought out all the anvils the town could muster, and taking up a collection to pay for powder proceeded to get all the noise possible out of them. Had there been any Indians anywhere in hearing they would probably have gotten away from that vicinity in short order.
>
> We felt something like the children of Israel probably did, when Jehovah flung the Red Sea betwixt them and

their foes. Judge Baylor, Baptist preacher though he was, made a full hand with the boys.

—

Smithwick, Noah, The Evolution of a State, Austin: Steck-Vaughn Company, 1968.

# JESSE STEM WAS KILLED BY A KICKAPOO

William Lepperman and former Indian agent Jesse Stem were killed by Kickapoo Indians near Fort Belknap, Young County, in February 1854.

Lieutenant Arthur D. Tree, of the United States Army, went in pursuit of the perpetrators. A $500 reward was offered for the arrest of the guilty parties; however, a Kickapoo tribal council had already acted.

William B. Parker wrote,

In a short time one of the murderers was arrested by his own people, firmly bound and placed on horseback to be taken into the fort. A short distance from that place he managed to free himself from his bonds, and throwing himself from the horse attempted to escape, but was immediately shot down and his dead body carried in and delivered to the officer in command.

The other made his escape, but after eluding pursuit for a time made his way to a village where his brother lived. Entering this he commenced exclaiming in a loud voice, "I am the murderer of Colonel Stem, will no one take me and deliver me up for punishment?" In this way he reached his brother's lodge, entering which, he said, "My brother, I committed this murder. I am tired of life. I am hunted down like a wild beast, and I want to die. I tried to join the Comanches but would have starved to death before I could have found them."

Food was set before him, of which he partook. His brother and he then walked out of the village, where the former said to him, "My brother, you have disgraced our tribe and it is my duty to kill you...." Stepping behind him he then felled him to the earth with his tomahawk, and with repeated blows dispatched him. A council was then held, at which the brother made a speech, stating what he had done, and why....

Not long after Jesse Stem was buried at Fort Belknap, his widow and children moved back to Sandusky, Ohio.

—

Matthews, Sallie Reynolds, <u>Interwoven</u>, Austin: University of Texas Press, 1958.

Parker, W. B., <u>Notes Taken During the Expedition Comandeed by Capt. R. B. Marcy, U. S. A., Through Unexplored Texas ...</u>, 1856.

# A NACOGDOCHES MURDERER DEMANDED PUNISHMENT

Nacogdoches may be the oldest city in Texas, for the Spaniards established their Mission Guadalupe at an existing Indian town. The fortunes of Nacogdoches waxed and waned throughout the Spanish and Mexican periods, and the population was about one hundred in 1822, when William Dewees visited there. He wrote,

> The town was nearly destroyed in the revolution of 1812, since which it has not been rebuilt, and of course is a very desolate looking place. The buildings consist of a large stone church, another large stone building with eight or ten apartments in it. What it was constructed for, I am unable to say, but at the present time it is occupied by several families. The remainder of the buildings are adobes, except a few which are made of wood.

While Dewees was in Nacogdoches, a stranger begged the commander to hang him for murder. The Spanish officials and the citizenry considered him deranged. The stranger claimed that he and his partner had returned from a trading trip to Mexico, and he killed the associate, took his money, and dumped the body into the Angelina River. To pacify the poor fellow — who made a pest of himself by repeatedly confessing his offense and demanding punishment — the colonel sent a search party to the river, where the body of the murdered partner was found.

Apparently, the commandant saw no need for a trial. Instead, he assembled witnesses, "took the man out behind the old stone building, and there, according to the man's request, hung him upon a tree till he was dead."

In Nacogdoches, Dewees learned about Moses Austin's Texas venture. (Austin, of Potosi, Missouri, had obtained official permission to bring in settlers.) Dewees became a colonist in the Austin grant.

—

Dewees, W. B., Letters From an Early Settler of Texas, Louisville, Kentucky: Morton and Griswold, 1852.

# FOR HALF A SUNDAY SAN ANTONIO MOURNED DANIEL WEBSTER

When Frederick Law Olmsted visited San Antonio, in 1854, he estimated the population to be 10,500 — about 4,000 natives of Mexico, 3,000 Germans, and 3,500 former residents of the United States.

Of the Alamo, Olmsted wrote:

> It is now within the town and in extent probably a mere wreck of its former grandeur. It consists of a few irregular stuccoed buildings huddled against the old church in a large court surrounded by a rude wall, the whole used as an arsenal by the U. S. quartermaster. The church door opens on the square and is meagerly decorated by stucco mouldings all hacked and battered in the battles it has seen. Since the heroic defense of Travis and his handful of men in '36 it has been a monument not so much to faith as to courage.

Olmsted noted that, "A scanty congregation attends the services of the battered old cathedral. The Protestant church attendance can almost be counted upon the fingers."

The shrewd frugality of the city fathers amused Olmsted. While they had designated a day to mourn the death of Daniel Webster, no commercial opportunity was sacrificed in order to pay proper respects to the former United States Senator and Secretary of State. The city dads adopted this resolution:

> Be it resolved by the Board of Aldermen of the city of San Antonio in Common Council assembled, that, by

the death of the late Daniel Webster, the people are plunged in mourning, and in testimonial of our grief we sincerely join with other cities and towns of our country in requesting a suspension of labor, and the closing of all places of business on Sunday ... from 10 o'clock A . M. to 4 o'clock P. M., and that all the flags in the city be displayed at half-mast, and minute guns fired through the day.

—

Olmsted, Frederick Law, A Journey Through Texas, Austin: University of Texas Press, 1978.

# GOVERNOR SMITH DIED IN THE CALIFORNIA GOLD FIELDS

Henry Smith was born in Kentucky shortly before George Washington became president. He moved to present Brazoria County, Texas, in 1827. Smith believed that from the enactment of the Law of April 6, 1830 the government of Mexico intended to destroy the Texas settlements. "She feared their increasing power and intelligence and had secretly determined to oppress or exterminate [the settlers]."

After President Antonio Lopez de Santa Anna set aside the Constitution of 1824 and instituted military rule in Mexico, a consultation met to decide upon a course for Texas. Not long after the fighting began at Gonzales, delegates defeated an independence effort by voting, thirty-three to fifteen, to remain in the Mexican union and seek restoration of the constitution. The delegates elected Henry Smith provisional governor of Texas, by a vote of thirty-one to twenty-two, over Stephen F. Austin, who was then sent to raise money in the United States for the defense of Texas settlers. Sam Houston was to organize an army.

Smith's feuds with the council left Texas without an effective government as Santa Anna's army marched northward. At Washington-on-the-Brazos, delegates adopted a declaration of independence, on March 2, 1836, and elected David G. Burnet ad interim president.

Smith was Burnet's secretary of the treasury and a legislator before he joined the gold rush. He died in a mining camp near Los Angeles.

Henry Smith married three times — to sisters. The first wife, Harriet Gillet, bore three sons. After her death, Smith married Elizabeth Gillet, who gave him five daughters and died in a cholera epidemic. By Sarah Gillet — Elizabeth's twin — Smith had another daughter.

—

Johnson, Frank W., <u>A History of Texas and Texans</u>, Eugene Barker, ed., Chicago: American Historical Society, 1914.

# HENDERSON REPRESENTED THE REPUBLIC IN EUROPE

The first governor of the American state of Texas, James Pinckney Henderson, was a North Carolina native. A graduate of Chapel Hill College, he was admitted to the bar in 1829. Frank Lubbock described him as,

> ... one of those magnetic men that impress you at first sight as being of no ordinary stamp. He was tall and rather delicate in appearance, with light hair, fair complexion, and fine grey eyes; affable, and sparkling all over with genuine vivacity.

Henderson's health was damaged by overwork as he studied law eighteen hours a day. Hoping a change of climate would help, he moved to Mississippi.

Upon learning of Santa Anna's invasion of Texas, Henderson raised a company of volunteers, but he arrived after Houston had prevailed in the battle of San Jacinto. President Houston made him Attorney General and — after Stephen F. Austin's death — Secretary of State.

At age twenty-nine, Henderson became the Republic's minister to England and France. He was to obtain recognition of the new nation and negotiate commercial treaties. In London, Henderson married 19-year-old Frances Cox, of Philadelphia. She had lived in Paris, was fluent in eighteen languages and was competent in seven others.

Completing his European assignment, Henderson brought his bride home to a log house in San Augustine, Texas, where he opened a law office. Friends urged him to run for the presidency

— Lamar could not succeed himself — but he was not yet thirty-five, the minimum age prescribed by the constitution. (No doubt, he was cheered by those who claimed he appeared to be at least forty.)

—

Kittrell, N. G., <u>Governors Who Have Been and Other Public Men</u>, Houston: Dealy-Adey-Elgin Company, 1921.

Lubbock, Francis, <u>Six Decades in Texas</u>, Austin: Pemberton Press, 1968.

# HENDERSON COMMANDED TEXAS TROOPS IN BATTLE

In 1844, President Sam Houston asked James Pinckney Henderson to help Isaac Van Zandt negotiate annexation to the United States. Although Secretary of State John Calhoun recommended the treaty, the Senate rejected it. The Americans reacted by electing James K. Polk president and annexing Texas.

The leading candidates for the governorship of Texas were Dr. James B. Miller and Anson Jones' vice president Kenneth Anderson. A native of Henderson's North Carolina hometown, Anderson was the law partner of Henderson and Thomas Jefferson Rusk. During his campaign, Anderson died at Alta Mira, Grimes County. (The town was renamed Anderson in his honor.)

Henderson entered the governor's race and won. He was called "the elegant J. Pinckney" to distinguish him from James Wilson Henderson, Texas' fourth governor.

The first battle of the Mexican War was fought on April 25, 1846 near present Brownsville. After General Zachary Taylor requested four Texas regiments, the legislature complied and authorized the governor to command them. Henderson notified Lieutenant Governor Albert Clinton Horton that,

> I shall this day leave the seat of government to take command of the Texas forces raised under the requisition of General Taylor and shall move beyond the Rio Grande into Mexico. Under these circumstances, you are required by the Constitution to act as governor....

Taylor designated Henderson, General William J. Worth — for whom Fort Worth was named — and Colonel Jefferson Davis to negotiate the Mexican surrender after the battle of Monterey. On December 13, 1846, Henderson resumed his duties as governor. At the end of his term, he went home to San Augustine.

After a man threatened to shoot him, Henderson, told an acquaintance that he had not harmed the fellow. The friend said, "He will kill you all the same."

"But I have a family to support.... What shall I do?

The friend said, "Kill him."

Judge Norman G. Kittrell — for whom Normangee was named — wrote:

> ... the general acted upon the tragic suggestion and "removed" the man who was preparing to assassinate him; and calmly proceeded to the courthouse and entered upon the trial of a case. He was justified both by public sentiment and the law and no reproach attached to his action.

Appointed to the Senate seat of Tom Rusk, Henderson died seven months later. At the time of the Texas Centennial, no descendent of the first governor resided in the state. Most of his heirs lived in Europe, where the $1,500 ceremonial sword given him by Congress was situated in World War II.

—

Kittrell, N. G., <u>Governors Who Have Been and Other Public Men</u>, Houston: Dealy-Adey-Elgin Company, 1921.

Lubbock, Francis, <u>Six Decades in Texas</u>, Austin: Pemberton Press, 1968.

# GOVERNOR WOOD WAS A JUST MAN

Georgia-born George T. Wood raised a company for service in the Creek War. He may have met Ensign Sam Houston during that campaign.

Frank Lubbock considered Wood a fine-looking man. He was of more than medium height and strong and vigorous in appearance; however, his best-remembered personal characteristic was an aversion to wearing socks.

Wood came to Texas in 1836 and cleared land for a plantation on the Trinity River near Point Blank, in San Jacinto County. A congressman of the Republic of Texas and militia brigadier general, he was a colonel of volunteers during the Mexican War.

A controversy involving Major General James P. Henderson — on leave from his duties as governor of Texas — brought Wood's former subordinates to his assistance. Henderson's mistreatment of Wood may have caused voters to make Wood the state's second governor.

First ladies did not accompany their husbands to the frontier capital then. Mrs. Wood managed the plantation, and the governor boarded at Bullock's Hotel in Austin.

Wood rode his mule, Pantalette, to and from Point Blank, camping wherever night caught him and using his saddle for a pillow. The governor would put a loop around Pantalette's neck and tie the other end of the rope to his own ankle.

Wood's daughter could not recall a meal at their home without guests present. The governor's slaves regularly cultivated the fields of a sick and destitute neighbor. When Wood died, that unfortunate declared, "Well, daughter, the poor man's friend is gone."

Governor Wood died in Panola County about 1856; he is buried near Point Blank beneath a stone bearing the inscription, "Here sleeps a just man."

—

Kittrell, N. G., Governors Who Have Been and Other Public Men, Houston: Dealy-Adey-Elgin Company, 1921.

Lubbock, Francis, Six Decades in Texas, Austin: Pemberton Press, 1968.

# PETER BELL NEVER
# RETURNED TO TEXAS

P eter Hansborough Bell — whose statue dominates Belton's courthouse square — was perhaps the most picturesque Texas governor. Frank Lubbock described him as,

> ... a Virginian — a fine type of Southern gentleman, a well-built, handsome young fellow when he landed in Texas. He displayed much pluck and determination in participating as a private in the battle of San Jacinto. He was always affable and kind; became popular; rose rapidly in public estimation; commanded a company of rangers at an early day; fought bravely at Monterey as lieutenant-colonel in Wood's regiment, and then became Governor of Texas.

The tall, slender Bell kept his black hair collar-length, gunfighter-style. On ranger duty he was booted and spurred, wore a wide sombrero, and had two pistols and a Bowie knife on his belt. In town, Bell affected well-cut coats that came nearly to the knee and was "elegant and dignified."

John Henry Brown believed that Governor Bell "had not an enemy in Texas." In his second term, Bell was elected to Congress.

On March 3, 1857, Congressman Bell married Mrs. Ella Reeves Eaton Dickens, of Littleton, North Carolina. No longer interested in politics — or the Lone Star State — he settled on his wife's Carolina plantation. Peter Bell never saw Texas again.

Learning that Bell had lost everything during the Civil War, Governor Jim Hogg suggested pensioning the destitute former governor. In 1891, the Texas legislature voted to pay the 83-year-old Bell $100 per annum. The bodies of Bell and his wife were moved to the Texas State Cemetery as part of the 1936 centennial observance.

—

Brown, John Henry, <u>History of Texas</u>, 1685-1892, St. Louis: L. E. Daniell, 1893.

Lubbock, Francis, <u>Six Decades in Texas</u>, Austin: Pemberton Press, 1968.

# ELISHA PEASE KNEW ALL ABOUT THE TEXAS REPUBLIC

Texas' first three-term governor, Elisha Pease, was — in the words of Francis Lubbock — "a fine constitutional lawyer, a great statesman, and a patriot of incorruptible integrity." Born in Enfield, Connecticut, on January 3, 1812, Pease attended Westfield Academy until, at age fourteen, he went to work in a general store.

In 1835, Pease moved to Bastrop, where he studied law under D. C. Barrett. Because of a minor speech impediment, Pease's partners tried his lawsuits.

A member of the "peace party" until Santa Anna threatened Texas, Pease took part in the minor altercation at Gonzales that began the Revolution. He was secretary to the provisional council, clerk of the committee that wrote the Republic's constitution, and comptroller in Houston's first presidency.

After annexation, Pease authored the state's probate code. Benjamin Miller believed that: "If any man knew at first hand the evolution of the government of the Republic of Texas, that man was E. M. Pease."

In 1850, Pease brought his bride, Lucadia Niles, from Connecticut. (The journey required nearly two months.) She contributed to the improvement of life in Brazoria, where she had the first carriage, the first sidewalk, and the first flower bed.

As the fifth governor, Pease urged the establishment of a general education system from elementary to college level. The effort to found a university failed because of supporters' inability to agree upon whether there should be one institution or two.

Governor Elisha Pease was renowned for his memory. In 1883, <u>The Austin Daily Statesman</u> repeated a commonly-held belief that Pease "knew all the laws of Texas from statehood to the Civil War."

—

Kittrell, N. G., <u>Governors Who Have Been and Other Public Men</u>, Houston: Dealy-Adey-Elgin Company, 1921.

Lubbock, Francis, <u>Six Decades in Texas</u>, Austin: Pemberton Press, 1968.

# MRS. PEASE DID NOT WANT TO LIVE IN THE MANSION

Austin's designation as the capital of Texas extended only to 1870, but construction of state buildings would help keep the government there permanently. Citizens would not tax themselves to move the capital if adequate facilities existed in Austin. That conviction encouraged the men who supported construction of the new stone capitol and the governors mansion.

Governor Elisha Pease — the first occupant of the mansion — planted a vegetable garden. His wife raised flowers. In February, she made lard and cured hams, after killing twelve hogs.

Mrs. Pease was proud of the carriage she brought from the East, although it was too low to clear the tree stumps in the streets. Sewing for three daughters took much of her time, but the family was prospering on the governor's $3,000 annual salary.

As Pease was leaving office at the end of his second term, he warned that Republican attacks on slavery were dividing the nation. During the Civil War, he did not participate in public affairs or practice law.

When Union general Philip Sheridan, the military commander of Texas, removed Governor James W. Throckmorton, on August 8, 1867, he appointed Pease as the thirteenth governor.

Pease did not move into the mansion during his third term. Union general J. J. Reynolds continued living there — an arrangement that had the enthusiastic approval of Mrs. Pease.

When he could no longer abide General Reynolds'

interference, Pease resigned, and Texas was without a governor for three months.

—

Kittrell, N. G., <u>Governors Who Have Been and Other Public Men</u>, Houston: Dealy-Adey-Elgin Company, 1921.

Lubbock, Francis, <u>Six Decades in Texas</u>, Austin: Pemberton Press, 1968.

# CLARK SUCCEEDED THE DEPOSED SAM HOUSTON

By a vote of 166 to 7, the Secession Convention dissolved the ties binding Texas to the United States. Among those resisting disunion was James Throckmorton, whose statue stands on McKinney's old courthouse square. Enthusiastic voters approved the secession ordinance, and convention delegates met upstairs in the old capitol to announce that Texas was no longer part of the federal union.

Governor Sam Houston's office was in the basement of the capitol. When he refused to take an oath to support the Confederate States of America, Lieutenant Governor Edward Clark, a native of Georgia, was sworn as his successor. John F. Kennedy wrote, in Profiles in Courage:

> The rumbling and contemptuous voices began again. The office of Governor of Texas, Confederate States of America, was declared to be officially vacant; and Lt. Governor Edward Clark, "an insignificant creature, contemptible, spry and pert," stepped up to take the oath. (A close personal and political friend elected on Houston's ticket, Clark would later enter the executive office to demand the archives of the state, only to have his former mentor wheel slowly in his chair to face him with the grandly scornful question: " And what is your name, sir?")

Clark had settled in Harrison County, Texas, in 1842. He was an Annexation Convention delegate and a member of General James P. Henderson's staff during the Mexican War.

Responding to congratulations upon her son's new office,

Clark's mother stated,

> It is natural to have governors in my family. The dress I have on now was worn at my father's inaugural ball in Georgia, later at my husband's inaugural ball in the same state.

In 1861, Francis Lubbock frustrated Clark's attempt to win a second term, by 124 votes. As a Confederate brigadier general, Clark was wounded in action. He lived in Mexico for awhile after the war, and later he practiced law at Marshall.

—

Kennedy, John F., <u>Profiles in Courage</u>, New York: Harper, 1956.

Kittrell, N. G., <u>Governors Who Have Been and Other Public Men</u>, Houston: Dealy-Adey-Elgin Company, 1921.

Lubbock, Francis, <u>Six Decades in Texas</u>, Austin: Pemberton Press, 1968.

# LUBBOCK WAS NOT AT SAN JACINTO

An especially useful early Texan was Francis Lubbock, the older brother of the Confederate lieutenant colonel for whom the City of Lubbock was named. He lived an exciting eighty-nine years.

As a boy, in South Carolina, Lubbock met the Marquis de Lafayette when the old hero made his sentimental journey to the country he had helped birth. Lafayette's ship arrived after dark, and

> A procession was formed to receive our distinguished guest. I was in the line, carrying a sperm candle in each hand.... I had the honor of being presented to the illustrious general.

Lubbock lived into the age of flight.

His seventeen-year-old brother, Tom, moved to Texas during the Revolution, and, a few months later, Francis went in search of Tom. He brought a stock of groceries with him and sold the first barrel of flour and the first sack of coffee ever marketed in Houston.

Lubbock almost became mayor of the hamlet. He wrote, "though I did not accompany Columbus when he discovered America... I was certainly in at the discovery of Houston...." At first, Lubbock and his fellow passengers did not recognize the new town as they sailed up Buffalo Bayou.

Lubbock's two-room house in Houston had no windows, and

> When light and air were wanted, a board was knocked

off. A few rough boards were laid down for the floor, not extending under the bed.

President Houston appointed the twenty-two-year-old Lubbock as Comptroller of the Republic. "Houston was always kind to young men; most certainly he was in a great degree to me," Lubbock recalled.

While Lubbock was considering the purchase of a ranch near Harrisburg, Patrick Jack advised him, "Do not go into ranching; the business is not respectable."

Lubbock replied, "I believe, judge, I will go into the business to give it respectability."

In 1857, Lubbock was elected lieutenant governor over Jesse Grimes, as Hardin R. Runnels defeated Sam Houston for the governorship. Lubbock and Houston remained personal friends, even though they were political opponents.

Lubbock won the governorship from Edward Clark. Before taking office, he consulted Confederate officials to see how Texas could best assist the war effort. Returning home from Richmond by boat, Lubbock saw on the deck of an approaching troopship a young lieutenant colonel; it was his brother, Tom. Lubbock wrote,

> We recognized each other and signaled a farewell, I going to Texas to my duties as governor, and he, as a soldier, to meet the invaders at the threshold of our Southland. That was our last greeting on earth.

Thomas Lubbock — for whom the South Plains county is named — died soon after taking command of his regiment.

Francis Lubbock spent a difficult two years trying to govern Confederate Texas. At the November 1863 inauguration of his successor, Pendleton Murrah, Lubbock wore the uniform of a Confederate lieutenant colonel for the first time.

As a member of Jefferson Davis' staff, when the Confederacy fell, Lubbock was captured with the Southern president in Georgia. He was imprisoned at Fort Delaware, along with General Joe Wheeler. (Postmaster General John Reagan and Vice President Alexander Stephens were confined at Fort Warren in Boston harbor. Davis was imprisoned at Fortress Monroe for two years.)

The barred windows of Lubbock's 12-by-14-foot prison cell overlooked a moat. He recalled that,

> There was no chair or bed or blanket to rest upon, or indeed any article of furniture ... and there was no light except that furnished by the lamp in the hall. I used my saddle-bags for a pillow, and my Mexican blanket, which I had kept them from robbing me of, to sleep upon.

A member of Holland Lodge, at Houston, Lubbock received better treatment after the prison commander learned that he was a Mason. He got home to Texas on December 16, 1865.

Judge Norman G. Kittrell described Lubbock as

> ... an absolutely honest man and was a bright, catchy, and amusing speaker on the stump .... He swore like a trooper, but ... forsook that habit a number of years before he died, and joined the Presbyterian Church. Frank Lubbock carried the baby daughter of Jefferson Davis, later known as "the Daughter of the Confederacy," in his arms to visit her father when he was a prisoner at Fortress Monroe.

—

As state treasurer — and a near-legendary Texan — Lubbock told a veterans meeting,

> A great many people think I was in the battle of San Jacinto .... I am sorry, now, that I was not in the battle;

for, if I had been , my Texas record would now be complete. And, really, if I had known how few of you would have been killed, I would most certainly have been there.

In 1903, sixty-eight years after his first wedding, Lubbock married for the third time. Of life in the Republic, he recalled,

In truth, society in Houston at that early day, mixed though it was with some rough characters, and without the sheen of later finery, was just glorious; and I was young. I wonder if I am yet old.

—

Kittrell, N. G., Governors Who Have Been and Other Public Men, Houston: Dealy-Adey-Elgin Company, 1921.

Lubbock, Francis, Six Decades in Texas, Austin: Pemberton Press, 1968.

# GOVERNOR MURRAH FLED TO MEXICO

No one became governor of Texas at a worse time than the tenth man to hold that office, Pendleton Murrah, a South Carolinan and Brown University graduate. Murrah practiced law in Marshall, the secessionist capital of Texas.

After Francis Lubbock did not seek reelection, in 1863, Murrah defeated T. J. Chambers to become chief executive of Confederate Texas. Described as "a man of modest and gentle demeanor and of rather frail physique," in fact, Murrah was dying of tuberculosis. During his 16-month tenure, the war went badly, and the impoverished state and Confederate governments squabbled over the meager assets.

Following General Robert E. Lee's surrender at Appomattox, General Kirby Smith — unable to contact Confederate officials — requested the counsel of the governors of Louisiana, Texas, Missouri, and Arkansas. Too ill to attend the May 9, 1865 meeting at Marshall, Murrah sent Guy Bryan to represent Texas. General Smith surrendered at Galveston on June 2.

According to John Henry Brown,

> Texas was again in a state of chaos. Governor Murrah called in vain upon the state officers to protect public property, and on the same day, he performed the ceremony of ordering, by proclamation, a re-assembling of the legislature ....

Aware that the victors had imprisoned President Jefferson Davis, Governor Letcher, of Virginia, and Governor Moore, of Alabama, Murrah fled across the Rio Grande. Broken in health, spirits, and fortune, Murrah died in Monterey in August of 1865. General Jo Shelby wrote, "He knew death was near to him, yet he put on his old gray uniform, mounted his old war horse, and rode away, dying in Mexico."

—

Brown, John Henry, <u>History of Texas, 1685-1892</u>, St. Louis: L. E. Daniell, 1893.

Kittrell, N. G., <u>Governors Who Have Been and Other Public Men</u>, Houston: Dealy-Adey-Elgin Company, 1921.

Lubbock, Francis, <u>Six Decades in Texas</u>, Austin: Pemberton Press, 1968.

# JOHN KENNEDY WAS TO SPEND THE EVENING OF NOVEMBER 23 IN THE MANSION

Recognizing a duty to house President Sam Houston, the Congress of the Republic reimbursed some of his living expenses. In a later effort to provide an executive residence, the Congress purchased Francis Lubbock's house at Main and Preston streets in Houston. Lubbock wrote:

> While I was chief clerk of the House of Representatives President Houston was occupying a small rough log cabin about twelve by sixteen feet, with probably a small shed attached. There was no fireplace—nothing but a small clay furnace in the room for him to get over and warm his fingers, Indian fashion.

> The question of securing a residence at once for the president was proposed in Congress, the friends of the measure urging the immediate necessity in consequence of his great discomfort. The government was about to issue a new currency. To the committee appointed to purchase a residence I proposed to sell for $6000 my store, a large old-time one-story house and a half story above, with dormer windows, if they would pay me for it out of the first money issued, so that I could remit at once to New Orleans. I made the sale. I then remitted and paid my debts with the money at par. In a short time the issue went down to eighty cents on the dollar.

> During the next spring, Congress voted $3000 more for repairs; and when Lamar became President there was an additional appropriation of $5000 to complete,

repair, and furnish the executive mansion. As the capital was removed to Austin in the fall of 1839, President Lamar did not occupy this building long.

The president's Austin residence was a two-story, white frame located between 7th and 8th and San Jacinto and Brazos streets. Completed in 1839, it was furnished with whatever could be salvaged from the Houston house, which had been sold.

Refusing to occupy the mansion in 1841, Houston stated, "The present executive has no disposition to appropriate the same to his use on account of its ruinous condition...."

Mexican raids on San Antonio caused lawmakers to return the capital to Houston. Austin's streets were soon choked with weeds and the president's bat-infested residence was falling down.

Although the constitution of the State of Texas provided for an executive residence, nothing was done until 1854, when the legislature appropriated $14,500 — a sum that was to be raised from the sale of city lots.

A commission composed of Governor Elisha M. Pease, the Comptroller, and the Treasurer awarded the building contract to the lowest responsible bidder. The two-story, nine-room mansion was to measure 48 feet by 56 feet. Each room was to have a fireplace and the mansion's six Ionic columns would be made of cedar logs hauled by slaves from Bastrop.

Abner Cook, the contractor, agreed to complete the house before Christmas of 1855. When he did not meet the deadline, Cook was penalized $435 for the five months and twenty-four days in which other housing had to be provided for Governor Pease.

S. M. Swenson — the Austin merchant who founded the SMS ranches in West Texas — spent the $2,500 appropriated for furnishings on tables and chairs for the dining room and furniture for two parlors, a bedroom, and a hall.

After women criticized Swenson's failure to buy anything for the kitchen, the commissioners recommended the purchase of glassware, tableware, and cooking utensils, as well as furniture for the other four bedrooms. They also requested funds to dig a well and landscape the grounds.

In addition, they sought legislative approval for having erected the mansion on the wrong lot.

Moving in during 1856, Pease threw a party that he believed was

... the best one ever got up in Austin. The Ladies turned out well, there was a perfect jam ... there were present at different times...at least five hundred persons.... It was the first Public party ever given by a Governor of Texas.

The mansion's first century was a succession of crises. The building fell apart, its furnishings were wrecked and lost, and appropriations for repairs and replacements were wholly inadequate.

When Governor Runnels listed the mansion's needs for the legislature, a Democrat claimed new furniture would be wasted on incoming Governor Sam Houston, who was "accustomed to no more than a wigwam."

Robert E. Lee, a distant kinsman of Mrs. Houston, visited at the mansion just before the Civil War. Later, while across the road in the capitol the Secession Convention was tabulating the votes cast on the ordinance of secession, Houston — who had campaigned passionately against disunion — waited on the mansion's front porch. After a few weeks, he was deposed for refusing to take the Confederate oath of office.

The mansion is Austin's oldest public building. In 1949, Mrs. Allan Shivers noted that the wallpaper flapped with the winds. The plumbing and heating pipes were exposed, and during a rain she would "go down to the kitchen for pans to catch the water — it wasn't just a drip; it poured." In May of 1957, a twenty-four-pound piece of plaster fell from the ceiling during a reception.

Mrs. James Ferguson considered her impeached husband vindicated when Texas elected her governor and the family returned to the residence at the commencement of her first term.

In the Sam Houston room were born Temple Houston, in August of 1860, and Sam Houston Allred, during the Great Depression. That room has been occupied by presidents and rulers of foreign nations.

The Houston bed was too soft for John Kennedy's bad back, so Governor Price Daniel switched rooms with him one evening in 1960. President Kennedy was to spend the night of November 22, 1963 at the mansion, but he was killed — and Governor John Connally was wounded — in Dallas that day.

—

Lubbock, Francis, Six Decades in Texas, Austin: Pemberton Press, 1968.

# BURNET WAS THE AD INTERIM PRESIDENT

Believing he was dying of tuberculosis, David G. Burnet came to Texas in 1817, when, as A. M. Hobby described it,

> ... the entire Anglo-American population of this vast country, from the Sabine to the Rio Grande, and from the coast to the Rocky Mountains, did not exceed a hundred souls. From Nacogdoches to San Antonio the smoke of no human habitation arose.

Burnet lived for two years with a band of Comanche on the Colorado River.

> He slept without shelter through the vicissitudes of the seasons, and subsisted entirely on wild game. The food, exercise and climate of that delightful and invigorating region repaired the wastes of disease, renewed his physical energies and restored him to vigorous health. To the active habits of his hunter life during his stay may be ascribed, not only his cure, but his longevity and subsequent exemption from disease.

Burnet's father, an army surgeon and friend of George Washington, was a member of the Continental Congress; his older brother, Jacob, was a United States Senator from Ohio, and another brother, Isaac, was the Cincinnati mayor whose constituents gave Texians the pair of six-pounder cannon — the "Twin Sisters" — used in the battle of San Jacinto.

Giving up his Cincinnati law practice, David Burnet returned to Texas in 1826. After the convention at Washington-on-the-Brazos declared Texas to be independent of Mexico, Burnet was elected ad interim president of the Republic — an unenviable position. The Alamo had fallen, Santa Anna's army was on the move, the penniless government was in danger of capture, and the population was in flight.

After moving the capital to Harrisburg, Burnet fled. Colonel Almonte reached the beach as Burnet was crossing to Galveston Island. Standing in a boat rowed by two men, and holding one of his children, Burnet was within range of his pursuers; but Almonte would not permit his men to shoot, because "there was a mother and children on the boat."

The government sojourned in Galveston, Velasco, and Columbus. Burnet dealt with problems as well as he could. The stubborn Burnet lived 82 years. Ashbel Smith believed him to be "a man John Knox would have hugged with grim delight."

—

Clarke, Mary Whatley, David G. Burnet, Austin: Pemberton Press, 1969.

De Cordova, Jacob, Texas: Her Resources and Her Public Men, Philadelphia: J. B. Lippincott, 1858.

De Shields, James P., They Sat In High Place, San Antonio: Naylor Publishers, 1940.

Sloan, Sallie Everett, "The Presidential Administration of David G. Burnet, March 17 - October 22, 1836, With a Sketch of His Career," M. A. thesis, University of Texas at Austin, 1918.

# LAMAR WAS A PRINCELY TROUBADOR

The Georgia-born Mirabeau Bonaparte Lamar succeeded Sam Houston as president of the Republic. Ashbel Smith believed him to be a "princely troubador" who "knew not the emotion of personal fear." Frank Lubbock left this description:

> He was a man of French type, 5 feet 7 or 8 inches high, with a dark complexion, black hair, inclined to curl, and grey eyes. Lamar was peculiar in his dress; wore his clothes very loose, his pants being of that old style, very baggy and with large pleats, looking odd, as he was the only person I ever saw in Texas in that style of dress.... [He was] rather reserved in conversation ... however ... quite companionable with his intimate friends.

At twenty-one, Lamar published The Cahawba Press at Alabama's capital—Cahawba, in Dallas County. While serving as secretary to Georgia's governor George M. Troup, Lamar helped entertain the Marquis de Lafayette at Savannah. Although he was an attorney, Lamar probably never practiced.

Lamar's first wife was the seventeen-year-old Tabitha Jordan, who died after four years, leaving an infant daughter. He lost a race for Congress, and his newspaper, The Columbus Enquirer, failed. Ill and depressed, in 1835, Lamar moved to Washington County, Texas.

An early advocate of independence, Lamar joined Houston's army as a private soldier. On the eve of the battle of San Jacinto, he discovered that the enemy had surrounded Secretary of War Thomas J. Rusk and Colonel Walter Lane. Of their rescue, Philip

Graham wrote,

> Killing one Mexican lancer, and putting the others to flight, Lamar extricated his comrades-in-arms. Legend adds that he then coolly rode in front of the Mexican lines back to his own squad, the enemy acknowledging their admiration by a volley as he passed, and he reining in his horse and bowing in reply.

Next day, when the Texans vanquished Santa Anna's army, Lamar was a colonel of cavalry.

President David G. Burnet made him Secretary of War, but when Lamar tried to assume command of the army, the troops rejected him. His embarrassment on that occasion may have caused voters to elect him vice president.

Lamar was so lionized during a visit to Georgia that he decided to run for the presidency of the Texas republic. His main opponents in the race to succeed Houston were Peter William Grayson — who shot himself on July 9, 1838 — and James Collinsworth — who drowned in Galveston Bay that same month. (Grayson County is situated north of Dallas on Red River, as is Lamar County. Collingsworth — the legislature spelled his name incorrectly — County is on the Plains.)

Lamar then defeated the sole remaining candidate, Robert Wilson, by 6,695 ballots to 252. He and Vice President David G. Burnet were inaugurated on December 10 at the old Houston capitol, which occupied the site of the Rice Hotel. (Houston's population was then about 1,500.)

Lamar and Houston feuded and narrowly avoided fighting a duel. Herbert Gambrell wrote:

> While "Old Sam Jacinto" was holding court in his dirt floor cabin, Lamar gathered about him in the "White House" of the Republic an entourage which Houston dubbed "the Court of King Witumpka."

Phillip Graham observed that,

> The two men were symbolic of different civilizations:
> Lamar, of the Old South, its culture and traditions;
> Houston, of the new frontier of the Southwest in its
> most victorious mood.

---

Mirabeau Bonaparte Lamar's family was noted for unusual names. His brother was Lucius Quintus Cincinnatus Lamar, and his nephew, Lucius Quintus Cincinnatus Lamar, Jr., was United States Senator from Mississippi and Associate Justice of the United States Supreme Court. His leadership after the Civil War earned him the sobriquet — "the noblest Mississippian of them all."

The source of the unusual names was an unmarried uncle who had seized the privilege of naming nieces and nephews. He worked his magic upon several defenseless children — including Gazaway Bugg Lamar. Later, he married a woman who would not tolerate the kind of nonsense for which he was famed, and his children were blessed with quite ordinary names.

---

Because Lamar advocated the establishment of schools, he has been considered the father of Texas public education. In 1839, the Congress gave each county three leagues of land in support of its educational efforts, and fifty leagues were set aside to support two universities—the University of Texas and Texas A&M—both of which were established much later. Upon Lamar's suggestion, Congress authorized the state library.

Lamar was responsible for moving the capital from Houston. The site commission chose Waterloo, a tiny Colorado River settlement of half a dozen residents. Lamar, on a hunting trip, had been impressed by the beauty of the location.

The commission said the area was "a region worthy of being the home of the brave and free." By the time the government was installed, in October, 1839, the town had been named for Stephen Austin. Congress first met there in November 1840.

—

Graham, Philip, The Life and Poems of Mirabeau B. Lamar, Chapel Hill: University of North Carolina Press, 1938.

Lubbock, Francis, Six Decades in Texas, Austin: Pemberton Press, 1968.

Murphy, James. B., L. Q. C. Lamar: Pragmatic Patriot, Baton Rouge: Louisiana State University Press, 1973.

# PRESIDENT JONES WAS A PHYSICIAN

Anson Jones was a Massachusetts native. (His father had participated in the battle of Bunker Hill.) Licensed as a physician in New York, Jones practiced in Philadelphia before moving to New Orleans, where he found the "pernicious habits of gambling ... growing upon me.... I also found myself learning to imitate the fashionable habit of taking a 'julip' much oftener than was at all necessary."

In October 1833, Dr. Jones landed in Texas, immediately discovered his mistake, and decided to return to New Orleans. With assets of $17, in cash, and medicine worth $50, his debts exceeded $2,000.

While waiting for a ship, Jones was persuaded to hang out his shingle at Brazoria, and the practice prospered sufficiently to keep him in Texas. By 1835, Jones had built,

> ... a practice worth in money and available property about five thousand dollars a year, with a prospect of its increasing; and had I continued at my business, and not been induced to join the army and go into public life, I might and probably would at this time have been worth an independent fortune....

After the Alamo fell — and while the Runaway Scrape was in progress — Jones joined the army. Although he was assigned as a physician, Jones insisted upon remaining a private soldier.

A close friend of Sam Houston, Jones recalled that during the San Jacinto campaign, General Houston

> ... asked me after supper, privately, what I thought of

the prospect. I told him the men were deserting and if the retreating policy were continued much longer he would be pretty much alone. He seemed thoughtful and irresolute. Said he hoped yet to get a bloodless victory....

—

Gambrell, Herbert, Anson Jones, The Last President of Texas, Austin: University of Texas Press, 1964.

Jones, Anson, Republic of Texas, Its History and Annexation, Chicago: Rio Grande Press, 1966.

# ANSON JONES RANG DOWN THE CURTAIN ON THE REPUBLIC

By 1,500 votes, Anson Jones defeated General Edward Burleson to succeed Sam Houston and become the last president of the Republic. Jones' main task was to effect annexation; however, it was important that he exercise extreme caution, for the Texians had been disappointed in past dealings with the United States. Because of his guarded statements, enemies charged Jones with obstructing annexation. He was never able to rid himself of the suspicion that he had resisted statehood.

On June 6, 1845, Jones presented the "propositions which had been made on the part of the United States," and they were accepted by the Texas Congress. A convention met on July 4, and by a vote of 55 to 1 — six delegates did not vote — passed an annexation ordinance. The lone dissenter was Richard Bache, Benjamin Franklin's grandson.

At Austin, President Jones proclaimed the death of the Republic on February 16, 1846. The capitol had been used as a church, school, and annexation convention hall in the four years since the government moved to Houston. Jones stated,

> The Lone Star of Texas, which ten years ago arose amid clouds over fields of carnage, obscurely seen for awhile, has culminated, and following an inscrutable destiny, has passed on and become fixed forever in that glorious constellation which all free men and lovers of freedom in the world must reverence and adore — the American Union.... The final act in the great drama is now performed. The Republic of Texas is no more!

As Jones lowered the flag, the pole broke.

Jones was the master of Texas' first Masonic body — Holland Lodge Number 36, at Brazoria. As Mexican troops approached, Jones kept the charter in his saddlebags for safekeeping. When the Grand Lodge of Texas was organized — with Sam Houston presiding — Jones was the Grand Master.

When both United States Senate seats fell vacant because of Thomas J. Rusk's death and legislative repudiation of Sam Houston, Jones hoped to be appointed. But he was ignored.

On January 9, 1858, in Houston's Capitol Hotel — the building that had accommodated the government of the Republic — Jones killed himself. He had told a friend, "Here in this house, twenty years ago, I commenced my political career in Texas, and here I would like to close it." His widow, Mary Smith Jones, died fifty years later.

—

Gambrell, Herbert, Anson Jones, The Last President of Texas, Austin: University of Texas Press, 1964.

Jones, Anson, Republic of Texas, Its History and Annexation, Chicago: Rio Grande Press, 1966.

# CHARLES LINDBERGH CRASHED INTO A HARDWARE STORE

Long before he became an international hero, Charles Lindbergh was well-known in part of Texas. (He would have given a far different meaning to the name Charles Manson if his grandfather, Ola Manson, had not changed his surname to Lindbergh upon arriving in the United States.)

Lindbergh had been obsessed by the desire to fly from the time he first saw an airplane. He enrolled in an aviation course, but the owners of the school—afraid that he might wreck their plane—would not let him attempt to fly alone.

In the next few months, he barnstormed, walking wings and making parachute jumps. (Motor trouble forced him down near a Wyoming buffalo herd.)

In 1923, Lindbergh bought a war surplus Curtiss Jenny. Although he had not soloed, he flew the aircraft from Georgia to Minnesota. His route was through Texarkana because, "While learning to fly in Nebraska the previous spring I discovered that nearly every pilot in existence had flown in Texas at one time or another...." At the new Texarkana airport, he landed among stumps.

Unable to get a license without a solo flight, and realizing that the Army offered the only opportunity to learn to fly the best planes, Lindbergh sold the Jenny and enlisted.

While he was waiting to begin basic training, Lindbergh met Leon Klink, who owned a Curtiss Canuck but did not know how to fly.

From St. Louis, Lindbergh and Klink flew to Florida, then turned westward, setting down in pastures where livestock constituted the great hazard. Because cattle enjoyed the taste of the painted canvas surfaces, they had to be restrained from chewing up the wings and tail.

At San Antonio's Brooks Field, Lindbergh verified his induction date. Having a few days to waste, he and Klink decided to fly to California.

In order to extend their range, they bought two extra cans of gasoline. When the extra weight kept them from rising above a hundred feet, Klink tossed one container overboard. Needing more altitude, Lindbergh had Klink jettison the second can.

Lindbergh and Klink were navigating by a railroad map, but neither was proficient in interpreting the primitive chart. They mistook the West Nueces for the Rio Grande, got lost, and ran out of gas near Barksdale, Texas.

Lindbergh made an emergency landing in a sheep pasture and hitched a ride on a farm wagon to buy gasoline. The refueled plane was too heavy to lift off from the small enclosure with both aboard, so Lindbergh flew over to Camp Wood and landed on the public square, while Klink made the trip on foot.

The Canuck generated more excitement than Camp Wood had known in decades, and the event demanded celebration. Lindbergh had intended to leave the next day, but Klink insisted upon remaining for the dance their visit had provoked.

Lindbergh wrote:

> One of the town streets was wide enough to take-off from, provided I could get a forty-four foot wing between two telephone poles forty-six feet apart and brush through a few branches on either side of the road later on. We pushed the ship over to the middle of the street and I attempted to take-off. The poles were about

fifty feet ahead and just before passing between them there was a rough spot in the street. One of the wheels got in a rut and I missed by three inches of the right wing tip. The pole swung the plane around and the nose crashed through the wall of a hardware store, knocking pots, pans and pitchforks all over the interior.

The merchant and his son thought that an earthquake was in progress and came running out into the street. He was highly pleased to find an airplane halfway into his place of business and not only refused to accept anything for damages, but would not even allow us to have the wall repaired. He said the advertising value was much more than the destruction.

By telegraph, Lindbergh ordered a new propeller; it arrived by freight train from Houston a couple of days later.

After Klink repaired the plane, they continued westward. At Maxon, Brewster County, they spent several hours clearing sagebrush and cactus from a field, but still the brush would not allow them to reach flying speed. Finally, a large Spanish dagger plant tore a hole in the left lower wing.

The engineer on a passing train saw what happened and permitted Klink to climb aboard. In El Paso, he bought materials to repair the torn wing fabric.

By the time the plane was airworthy, Lindbergh needed to report to Brooks Field. On March 14, 1924, he began training with 103 other aviation cadets.

His 1927 flight from New York to Paris made Lindbergh famous throughout the world. Probably no American has been so celebrated. Everyone knew "Lucky Lindy."

Some residents of the Edwards Plateau still remembered conversations with the famous flyer half a century after the visit.

Ask about Lindbergh in Camp Wood, and some old-timer was liable to answer, "Tall fellow! Right?"

—

Lindbergh, Charles A., The Spirit of St. Louis, New York: Scribners, 1952.

Lindbergh, Charles A., We, New York: Putnam, 1927.

# NEWTON AND JASPER WERE REVOLUTIONARY HEROES

Newton and Jasper counties are twin slivers of land located just below Sabine County, in East Texas. They honor Sergeant John Newton, of Charleston, South Carolina, and his good friend, Sergeant William Jasper, who was probably the most famous enlisted man of the American Revolution.

Jasper joined the company raised by Francis Marion, "The Swamp Fox." (Marion County, Texas, is named for him.) On June 28, 1776, Jasper was at Fort Sullivan — a military works of palmetto logs and sand built by Colonel William Moultrie — during a British naval bombardment. (That day Fort Sullivan was renamed Fort Moultrie.) An eyewitness described the action as "the most furious fire I ever saw or heard."

A British cannonball knocked down the flag under which the Americans were fighting — the word "Liberty" embroidered upon a blue field. Sergeant Jasper, ignoring heavy fire, leaped through an embrasure, tied the flag to the staff of a cannon sponger, and restored it to the ramparts — defying the enemy and signaling to friends that they still held out.

South Carolina president John Rutledge offered to commission Jasper for his bravery, but the sergeant declined because of fear that his illiteracy would embarrass him as an officer.

Three years later, Jasper and Newton fought at Savannah. As Jasper tried to plant his regiment's colors on the Spring Hill redoubt — where three others had fallen in the same effort — he was killed. Sergeant Newton was captured at Charleston in 1780 and died of smallpox.

Several states have named counties for Jasper and Newton, usually in association. (Sometimes the county honors one sergeant and the seat of government commemorates the other.) Newton County, Missouri—Neosho is the seat—adjoins Jasper County, where Carthage is the capital. Newton County, Texas, was carved from Jasper County, and they stand side by side, as did the two soldiers and friends more than two centuries ago.

—

# NAVARRO WAS THE STERN AND HONEST PATRIOT

A native of the Corsican town in which Napoleon was born, Angel Navarro came to Mexico as a soldier in the Spanish Army. After his discharge, he was the alcalde of San Antonio. Navarro fathered seven boys — all named Jose — and five girls with the name of Maria. His eighth child was Jose Antonio Navarro, a signer of the Texas Declaration of Independence.

As a member of the Santa Fe Expedition, Jose Navarro was captured in New Mexico and imprisoned in Mexico. President Antonio Lopez de Santa Anna, frustrated in his desire to execute Navarro, tried to kill him through neglect and harsh treatment. A fellow prisoner of the Santa Fe Expedition, George Wilkins Kendall, of the New Orleans Picayune, wrote that,

> Not content with simply depriving him of liberty the heartless tyrant kept him constantly confined in the vilest and most filthy prisons, and among the lowest malefactors. Over and over again was he offered liberty, station, and wealth if he would turn against Texas or use his influence to bring her back into the Mexican confederacy; but inflexibly pure, the stern and honest patriot spurned every effort with disdain.

For two years, Navarro was chained to the floor of a dungeon cell, but after Santa Anna fell from power, he was allowed the freedom of his island prison. Managing to escape, Navarro reached home in 1845, four years after leaving on the Santa Fe mission.

Annexation convention delegate Navarro was elected to the first state Senate. When his colleagues named a county for him, he wanted the seat of government to honor his father, Angel, the Corsican.

Jose Navarro died at San Antonio in 1871. The state has restored his San Antonio home and opens it to visitors each day. His statue sits on the Navarro County square in Corsicana.

—

Dawson, Joseph, Jose Antonio Navarro, Waco: Baylor University Press, 1969.

Kendall, George Wilkins, Narrative of the Texas Santa Fe Expedition, Washington, DC: 1850.

# STEPHEN AUSTIN FULFILLED HIS FATHER'S DREAM

No country ever had a more selfless founder than Stephen Fuller Austin. His father, after going broke in Missouri, had hoped to settle colonists in Texas, but Moses Austin died from the effects of his difficult journey to San Antonio. On his death bed, Moses requested that Stephen carry out the project.

Stephen Austin, twenty-seven, was an Arkansas district judge who had served six years in the Missouri territorial legislature. He was superbly qualified for his task. Well-educated for the time, experienced in government and business, Austin was methodical, patient, wise, and tactful. His compensation for years of hard work and privation in settling Texas was meager.

Austin was imprisoned and detained in Mexico for years after he presented a petition seeking Mexican statehood for Texas separate from Coahuila.

William Zuber wrote of standing in his doorway watching a horseman who sat motionless on his mount in a heavy rain. Zuber was only a boy. "That is Colonel Austin," his father said. Austin was waiting on friends who were to accompany him to Anahuac. Young Zuber ran out into the rain to get a better look, and years later, he wrote:

> He was small of stature. He wore a sealskin cap, with the reflex edges turned down to protect his ears, and a drab overcoat which covered him from head to foot, the collar being turned up to protect his neck, leaving his face exposed to view. We looked at each other, but neither spoke. After viewing him for about three minutes, I returned to the house, glad to get out of the

rain. Though I knew that this man was much admired by many persons, I had no idea of the magnitude of his character, nor dreamed of the sufferings which he was to endure for his country.

—

Gracy, David B. II, <u>Moses Austin: His Life</u>, San Antonio: Trinity University Press, 1987.

Zuber, William, <u>My Eighty Years in Texas</u>, Austin: University of Texas Press, 1971.

# JIM BOWIE WAS AT THE SANDBAR DUEL

———————

Jim Bowie was a legendary figure even before he came to Texas. The Kentucky-born Bowie grew up on frontiers in Missouri and Louisiana, where he was said to have roped and ridden alligators. Bowie smuggled slaves, searched for lost gold mines, and speculated in land. But it was a knife that made Bowie's name familiar to most Americans.

Bowie was once involved in a controversy with Sheriff Norris Wright, and each held a grudge against the other. In 1827, they were spectators at the notorious Sandbar Duel — an altercation that occurred on a strip of sand in the Mississippi River across from Natchez.

Each of the duel's principals had four seconds and a surgeon. A large crowd gathered on the sandbar, anxious to witness the blood-letting. Unfortunately — in the view of the spectators — the duelists settled their dispute without gunplay. That resolution pleased none of the audience, and a riot erupted. Men sought out their enemies and fell to working off grudges.

Having emptied their pistols, Bowie and Wright closed upon each other. Wright was armed with a cane sword, and Bowie carried a knife that had been made for his brother, Rezin. Wounded nine times, Bowie still was able to kill Wright.

Three years later, Arkansas blacksmith James Black designed a special knife for Jim Bowie. After Bowie was set upon by three robbers and successfully defended himself, everyone wanted such a knife.

The Bowie knife had a long, steel blade with an exaggerated, razor-sharp, curve near the point. A heavy handle provided balance. Useful mainly for display, it was extremely popular in the South and on the frontier.

A quarter century after Bowie died at the Alamo, Confederate soldiers took Bowie knives to the war. Those heavy weapons were discarded by the thousands as weary infantrymen finally shucked everything not absolutely essential to survival.

—

# ALPHONSO STEELE WAS THE LAST SURVIVOR OF SAN JACINTO

To excuse his poor performance in the battle of San Jacinto, on April 21, 1836, Santa Anna charged that Houston's army was composed of soldiers of fortune. That was far from the truth. Of the 877 officers and men on the muster rolls at San Jacinto, 707 definitely lived in Texas before independence was declared. Although it is impossible to determine when the other 170 arrived, no doubt many were Texas settlers before the Revolution.

Judge Seth Shepard wrote, "They came in good faith to make homes and to perform all the obligations of their compact and they did perform them as long as the central power permitted them to do so in peace and safety."

A typical San Jacinto veteran was Alphonso Steele, a Kentuckian who reached Texas in November of 1835. Steele, age nineteen, joined the army in March, 1836, and was one of the thirty-four Texans wounded at San Jacinto. Steele recalled that:

> I got my gun loaded and rushed on into the timber and fired again when the second volley was poured into them. In that timber they broke and ran. As soon as I got my gun loaded again I ran on a little in front of our men and threw up my gun to shoot when I was shot down. Dave Rusk was standing by me when I was shot. He told some of the men to stay with me but I told him, "No, take them on."

> One of our men in passing me asked if he could take my pistol but by this time I was bleeding at the nose and mouth so I couldn't speak, so he just stooped down and

got it and went on.

Steele and six other veterans attended the seventieth anniversary celebration of the battle of San Jacinto. Steele outlived the rest. He died July 7, 1911 at Mexia.

—

McDonald, Johnnie, "The Soldiers of San Jacinto," M. A. thesis, University of Texas at Austin, 1922.

# RICKENBACKER WAS A DALLAS CAR SALESMAN

Edward V. Rickenbacker was a racing driver who competed against Barney Oldfield and Louis Chevrolet. The leading World War I American flying ace, and a pioneer in commercial aviation, Rickenbacker was a Dallas car salesman at age eighteen.

Sent by the manufacturer to repair new automobiles that had failed in the Dallas heat, Rickenbacker solved the problem and remained to help the dealer market Firestone-Columbus cars. Rickenbacker used the testimony of a satisfied customer, a McLennan County physician, to close sales.

Another sure-fire marketing technique was climbing Chalk Hill in high gear. Rickenbacker wrote:

> We always made it, but one day, with a particularly heavy prospect aboard, I feared that we wouldn't. In an effort to give the buggy every chance, I made a running start and approached Chalk Hill at 30 miles an hour. The little buggy bounced and skidded on the gravel road like a skittish colt just learning to gallop. We started up the grade with my potential customer and me leaning forward and pushing with body English. Halfway up it became all too clear to me that we were not going to make it in high gear. Quickly I slammed on the brakes and we came to a dead stop .... I beamed at him with a proud smile. "How do you like those brakes?" I asked,. "See how they hold us tight, right here on Chalk Hill."
>
> He smiled back .... "Holy gee, that's great!" He bought the car that afternoon, for cash.

When Rickenbacker returned home after his year's work, he was five inches taller. His mother said, "My, they grow them big in Texas."

—

Rickenbacker, Edward V., Rickenbacker, Englewood Cliffs, NJ: Prentice-Hall, Inc., 1967.

# DAVY CROCKETT TOOK THE LONG WAY TO SAN ANTONIO

I used to doubt the claims made by some Texas towns that Davy Crockett had stopped there on his way to San Antonio. Then I read Pat Clark's account of the Crockett visit to Red River County and realized that I had unjustly suspected some city fathers of bending the truth. My error was in assuming that Crockett took a direct route across the state to San Antonio. That was not correct.

The former Tennessee congressman and his company crossed Arkansas Territory to Fort Towson, in present Oklahoma, and entered Texas at Jonesboro.

Crockett spent the first night in North Texas with an old friend, William Becknell. Because Crockett wanted to see a buffalo herd, his party borrowed mounts and, guided by Henry Stout, rode westward a hundred miles into virgin country. (West of John Robbins' Red River County cabin, Clark wrote, "so far as anyone knew," there was not a house "until reaching Mexico.")

There was no road — not even a path. Grass reached his saddle skirts as Crockett rode into present Fannin County, where bees were discovered nesting in the grass. The party camped near a flowing spring and some bee trees. Later, Crockett expressed a wish to settle at "the honey grove."

Returning to Becknell's place, Crockett was told about recent Comanche activity in the Texas interior and warned against traveling straight across the country to San Antonio de Bexar. A circuitous route was recommended, so the Tennesseeans rode eastward to Collin McKinney's home, near present Texarkana, then turned South. From Logansport, Louisiana,

Crockett's party followed El Camino Real through Nacogdoches to San Antonio.

The place where Crockett found honey bees nesting in the grass was later settled by Tennessean Samuel Erwin, who had been married by former Justice of the Peace David Crockett. Erwin gave the community the name Crockett had coined, and it remains Honey Grove to this day.

—

Clark, Pat, <u>Clarksville and Old Red River County</u>, Dallas: Mathis, Van Nort & Company, 1937.

# CHARLIE PADDOCK WAS THE WORLD'S FASTEST HUMAN

A few years ago, a fine motion picture about Olympic runners, —"Chariots of Fire"—won an Academy Award. The protagonists were British athletes, but numerous references were made to Charles Paddock, the great American sprinter.

Paddock was born August 11, 1900 in Gainesville, Texas, where his father was the Santa Fe Railroad station agent. Charles Paddock was a sickly child, and his parents, hoping a change of climate might help, moved to Southern California. There the boy outgrew his health problems and became an outstanding athlete at Pasadena High School and the University of Southern California. Representing the Los Angeles Athletic Club, Paddock won national American Athletic Union championships in 1920, 1921, and 1924 and set several world records.

In the 1920 Olympics, Paddock won gold medals in the 100 meters and the 400-meter relay, and he earned a silver medal in the 200-meter event. Although he had to settle for a silver medal in the 200 meters at the 1924 Olympics, Paddock was "the world's fastest human."

Five times Paddock ran the 100-yard dash in 9.6 seconds — equalling the world record — before running the first official 9.5 second, 100-yard dash in May of 1926.

Paddock had a distinctive running style and, as a journalist, he knew how best to handle his own publicity. For his many achievements, Paddock was elected to the Helms Track and Field Hall of Fame.

Paddock was an actor and movie producer. Early in World

War II, he joined the Marines, and on July 21, 1943, Captain Charles Paddock was killed in the crash of a Navy airplane near Sitka, Alaska.

—

Smith, A. Morton, The First 100 Years in Cooke County, San Antonio: The Naylor Company, 1955.

# ANDREWS WAS THE FIRST TEXIAN CASUALTY OF THE REVOLUTION

Richard Andrews, a big man noted for great strength, was at Gonzales in October of 1835, when the first shot of the Revolution was fired. (The Mexican commander of Texas had demanded the return of a small cannon furnished for Indian defense, but the people of Gonzales had refused to comply.)

Three weeks later, under Jim Bowie's command, Andrews took part in the battle of Concepcion, near San Antonio. Noah Smithwick recalled that Bowie, "a born leader," ordered everyone to stay under cover, and "had he been obeyed not a man would have been lost."

But Andrews, too "excited and eager to get a shot," was hit and lay "as he had fallen, great drops of sweat gathering on his white, drawn face, and the life blood gushing from a hole in the left side, just below the ribs."

Smithwick asked, "Dick, are you hurt?"

Andrews replied, "Yes, Smith, I'm killed; lay me down."

Later — ninety years old, blind, and living in California — Smithwick dictated the story to his daughter:

> I laid him down and put something under his head. It was the last time I saw him alive. There was not time for sentiment. There was the enemy, outnumbering us four to one, charging our position, so I picked up my gun and joined my comrades .... He recklessly, foolishly threw away his life, but his was the first freeman's life blood that wet the soil where the germ of the young

republic was just bursting into life.

Andrews was buried beneath a pecan tree near Mission Concepcion. The City of Andrews and Andrews County, in far western Texas, honor his memory.

—

Smithwick, Noah, <u>The Evolution of a State</u>, Austin: Steck-Vaughn Company, 1968.

# DOOLITTLE FLEW UNDER THE PECOS RIVER HIGH BRIDGE

James H. Doolittle was a special hero to many of us in Gainesville long before he led the 1942 raid on Tokyo. (Because the California-born Doolittle had lived in Alaska, the Nome Nugget headlined the story of the bombing of Japan, "NOME-TOWN BOY MAKES GOOD.")

Doolittle participated in General Billy Mitchell's demonstration of the potential of air power. He set speed and distance records, won races, and made the first instrument flight. The New York Times reported,

> Man's greatest enemy in the air, fog, was conquered yesterday at Mitchell Field when Lt. James H. Doolittle took off, flew over a 15-mile course and landed again without seeing the ground or any part of his plane but the illuminated instrument board.

Those were worthy accomplishments. We made balsawood models of the planes Doolittle flew to establish his records and followed his exploits in the newspapers. But in my crowd, Doolittle's fame rested upon our belief that he had flown beneath the High Bridge on the Pecos River.

When I began writing Texas books, I searched, without success, for information on Doolittle's alleged Pecos bridge feat. Finally, after some years, I gave up and did the obvious thing: I wrote a letter to General James H. Doolittle.

I was surprised by his prompt response and by the simple letterhead of the man who was really "Dr. Doolittle" by virtue of an earned doctorate and who was an Air Force lieutenant general and holder of the Congressional Medal of Honor. On the stationery, which bore only his name and address, Doolittle wrote,

> While flying Border Patrol out of Eagle Pass or Del Rio, I flew under the Pecos River High Bridge. This probably was in 1920. Have gone through my pilot book of the period, but note that I carefully avoided any mention of the event.
>
> The span of the bridge appeared barely wide enough to permit a DH-4 to fly through so I flew the shadow of the plane through first and found that it went through comfortably.
>
> As I approached the location of the bridge, flying quite low in the canyon, I noted a pair of telephone lines. I was, by this time, committed, so flew through the lines without incident, except for slight nicks in the propeller and forward struts.
>
> Heard later that the lineman who had to restring the telephone lines took a very dim view of the occasion.

—

Doolittle, James H., Los Angeles, letter to author August 27, 1976.

Glines, Carroll V., Jimmy Doolittle, Daredevil Aviator and Scientist, New York: Macmillan & Company, 1972.

# SAM HOUSTON BELIEVED TEXANS COULD MAKE A FLAG

---

Within weeks of his January 1829 marriage to the eighteen-year-old, blonde, blue-eyed Eliza Allen, Tennessee governor Samuel Houston, thirty-six, returned Eliza to her father's house in Gallatin. Resigning as governor, Houston left for the Cherokee Nation.

While living near Fort Gibson, in the Indian Territory, Houston became interested in Texas. He made his first journey south of Red River in 1832; he wrote President Andrew Jackson that Texans hoped the United States would purchase the province, because

> They are now without laws to govern or protect them. Mexico is involved in Civil War.... The people of Texas are determined to form a State Government and separate from Coahuila, and unless Mexico is soon restored to order and the Constitution revived and reenacted, the Province of Texas will remain separate from the Confederacy of Mexico.

Houston considered Texas the "finest country to its extent upon the globe .... the country east of the River Grande of the North would sustain a population of ten millions of souls."

In 1835, Nacogdoches citizens elected Houston to the Consultation. Given command of the army of farmers that would defend Texas, after an extended retreat before General Santa Anna's troops (despite the criticism of most Texians and the orders of President Burnet), he destroyed the Mexican army on the plain of San Jacinto.

Afterward, Santa Anna, the president of Mexico, tried to hide among the prisoners. Recognized and brought before Houston —who had been painfully wounded in the battle—he announced:

That man may consider himself born to no common destiny who has conquered the Napoleon of the West. It now remains for him to be generous to the vanquished.

Houston replied, "You should have thought of that at the Alamo."

In fact, Houston put himself in jeopardy more than once to protect Santa Anna, for he knew that the new nation would be discredited if harm came to the Mexican dictator.

Irritated over having been defeated by an army of untrained farmers, Santa Anna stated that Texas was without a governing body and —as additional evidence of incompetence—pointed out that it had no flag.

Houston replied that Texians believed they had a government, and "they will probably be able to make a flag."

—

James, Marquis, The Raven, Indianapolis: Bobbs-Merrill Company, 1929.

# THE SULTAN OF TURKEY CONTRIBUTED TO HOUSTON'S WARDROBE

Few Americans have held as many high offices as Sam Houston. In Tennessee, he was major general of militia, congressman, and governor. Houston commanded the Texas army, was president of the Republic, United States Senator, and governor of Texas. John Salmon "Rip " Ford described him as:

> ... a splendid specimen of manhood. A form and features which would have adorned the walks of royalty, a fund of conversational powers almost unequalled, the matchless gift of oratory, a vast grasp of intellect — all marked him a great man.

A Washington-on-the-Brazos resident left this recollection:

> On the crowded street was often seen Sam Houston, then President of the Republic and the central figure, whom many hated, some feared and all admired; a few loved him. I have seen him often at my father's house, and as evidence of his fondness for children he never saw one of us without recognition and some words of badinage. I frequently noticed him passing our door; ... always well-dressed and in appearance towering far above his fellows. I was particularly impressed by a splendid cloak he frequently wore. This cloak was of black velvet lined with yellow satin and the outside bound with ermine. He wore boots turned down from the top, lined with yellow silk and laced with yellow cords. These boots were called Wellingtons. The cloak was presented to him by some foreign potentate and

grandly did he wear it. His clothes need have cost him nothing, for his admirers were always giving him elegant things.

Dr. John Lockhart reported that,

The sultan of Turkey sent him a full suit of clothes as a present, consisting of a long flaming red robe of beautiful silk which came to near his ankles, pants of the regular Turkish fashion, large and baggy; around the waist they would measure several yards. They were intended to be gathered around the waist with a silk sash.... At the lower extremity shoes of yellow Turkish leather were sewed onto the pants.... General Houston could never be induced to try the pants on, but the robe was worn by him all summer in his office. It was made of the finest silk. The sultan also sent him a red fez to make the suit complete, but this he would never wear.

—

Friend, Llerena B., <u>Sam Houston, The Great Designer</u>, Austin: University of Texas Press, 1954.

James, Marquis, <u>The Raven</u>, Indianapolis: Bobbs-Merrill Company, 1929.

Wallis, Mrs. Jonnie L., <u>Sixty Years on the Brazos</u>, Waco: Texian Press, 1967.

# HOUSTON AND RUSK SPOKE FOR TEXAS

S am Houston and Thomas Jefferson Rusk were extremely able leaders. They assumed large responsibilities during and after the Revolution. On February 21, 1846, the legislature chose them to represent Texas in the United States Senate. Seventy votes were cast for Rusk and sixty-nine for Houston. (Lloyd Bentsen occupies the Rusk seat now, and Phil Gramm sits in Houston's chair.)

Following their election, Rusk and Houston met in Shelby County to plan for the future. When well-wishers would not leave them alone, the senators-elect climbed to the top of a sixteen-foot stack of lumber — taking along a jug of whiskey — and pondered the destiny of Texas.

During the Revolution, General Houston had continued a retreat despite orders to stop and fight Santa Anna. Finally, President Burnet sent Secretary of War Rusk to instruct Houston to make a stand. But Houston persuaded Rusk of the wisdom of his strategy, and Rusk joined the army, fought at San Jacinto, and succeeded the wounded Houston as commander.

On that retreat, Private S. F. Sparks invited Houston and Rusk to lunch on some chickens the soldier had acquired without purchase. Houston reprimanded Sparks for violating his rule against looting. The hungry general warned, "I'll not punish you for this offense, but if you are guilty of it a second time, I will double the punishment."

Rusk bit into the fried chicken and said, "General, it is a maxim in law that he who partakes of stolen property knowing it to be such is guilty with the thief."

Houston responded, "No one wants any of your law phrases, Rusk."

—

Friend, Llerena B., Sam Houston, The Great Designer, Austin: University of Texas Press, 1954.

James, Marquis, The Raven, Indianapolis: Bobbs-Merrill Company, 1929.

Sparks, S. F., "Recollections of S. F. Sparks," Quarterly of the Texas State Historical Association, XII (July 1908).

# HOUSTON WAS PRESIDENTIAL TIMBER

After taking the prescribed oath of office, the new senators from Texas drew lots to determine the length of their terms. Sam Houston received two years, and Thomas Jefferson Rusk got a six-year term.

Still serving in the Senate were Henry Clay, Daniel Webster, and Houston's bitter enemy, John Calhoun. Years before, Secretary of War Calhoun's unfounded charges had caused Lieutenant Houston to resign from the Army. (On the other hand, Rusk had been Calhoun's law student.)

President James K. Polk's diary entry of March 29, 1846 reflected a visit by Senator Houston. Polk was "much pleased to see him, having been with him in Congress twenty years ago and always his friend."

On April 23, 1846 — a decade after Houston defeated Santa Anna's army at San Jacinto — Mexico declared war on the United States. (Mexican politicians who claimed that Texas had not been lost in 1836 were embarrassed by annexation.)

Even after the battles of Palo Alto and Resaca De La Palma, on May 8 and 9, some critics, including Whig congressman Abraham Lincoln, refused to admit that the war existed.

Defending the Polk administration, on May 12, Houston pointed out that a state of war had existed between Mexico and Texas ever since 1836, and the United States had accepted Texas in that condition. As to the contention of Northern congressmen that Mexico owned the area between the Rio Grande and Nueces rivers, Mexico had never claimed the Nueces as its boundary; the

Mexicans claimed ownership of the entire state. Houston explained that, "Mexico insisted on her right as far as the Sabine, while Texas, by the right of conquest and independence, claimed from the Sabine to the Rio Grande."

In Washington, Senator Rusk devoted more energy than his colleague to serving constituents. Houston spent quite a bit of time traveling and making speeches, and many politicians — including Houston — considered him presidential timber.

—

Friend, Llerena B., <u>Sam Houston, The Great Designer</u>, Austin: University of Texas Press, 1954.

James, Marquis, <u>The Raven</u>, Indianapolis: Bobbs-Merrill Company, 1929.

# HOUSTON LOST HIS SENATE SEAT

$B$y 1847, when Sam Houston was reelected to the United States Senate, tensions over slavery were increasing rapidly. Old enemy John Calhoun, of South Carolina, criticized Houston for favoring Oregon legislation prohibiting slavery and organizing the territory as free soil.

Houston's support of the proposals that became the Compromise of 1850 angered Southerners, and his Senate career was ended by opposition to the Kansas-Nebraska Bill.

Senator Stephen A. Douglas, of Illinois, urged that residents decide whether a territory would be slave or free. Southern senators and congressmen believed this "squatter sovereignty" would expand slave territory, and most Texans favored Douglas' bill. Local determination of the slavery question would produce only strife, Houston contended. Denounced as a traitor by Texas newspapers, Houston urged retention of the Missouri Compromise line, for "The vast northwestern portion of our continent, unadapted to slave labor, will not be filled up by Southern men with slaves, and Northern people will increase their preponderance until the North is connected with California."

Houston warned, "Sir, if this repeal takes place, I will have seen the commencement of the agitation, but the youngest child now born will not live to witness its termination." Nevertheless, the House voted 113 to 100 for the Kansas-Nebraska Bill, and the Senate passed it, thirty-seven to fourteen. The only Southern senators who opposed the legislation were Houston and John Bell, of Tennessee. Although Houston still had five years remaining on his term, the legislature served notice that he would not be reelected.

As Houston predicted, slavery partisans from Missouri invaded Kansas to counter newcomers from the East. John Brown's outrages there were prologue to his Harpers Ferry, Virginia, raid — which seemed to offer Southerners proof that abolitionists would use force to free the slaves. Houston said,

> "I claim to be a Southern man. I was born in the South;
> I have served the South; I have been faithful to the
> South... but sir, I was born a man of the Union."

By destroying the Missouri Compromise, Houston believed the South "was inviting people to an uninhabited region to form a new State to be added to a section already numerically superior to her."

—

Friend, Llerena B., <u>Sam Houston, The Great Designer</u>, Austin: University of Texas Press, 1954.

James, Marquis, <u>The Raven</u>, Indianapolis: Bobbs-Merrill Company, 1929.

# SAM HOUSTON BECAME GOVERNOR

After the legislature denied his reelection to the Senate, Sam Houston ran for governor in 1857. He campaigned by buggy. Marquis James wrote:

> The summer was hot, and he would pull off his shirt and harangue the folk clad in a rumpled linen duster that reached from his neck to his ankles. He stirred the people.... He said things on the stump for which another man would have been shot. This appealed. A legendary hero had come to life—the weatherbeaten figure of "Old Sam Jacinto" himself, with a heart for any fortune and a hand for any fight.

Denied use of the Brenham courthouse, Houston said:

> I am not a taxpayer here. I did not contribute to buy a single brick or beam in this building and have no right to speak here. But if there is a man within the sound of my voice who desires to hear Sam Houston speak and will follow me hence to yonder hillside under the shade of yon spreading live oak, on the soil of Texas, I have a right to speak there because I have watered it with my blood.

But Hardin Runnels won. After suffering his only election defeat, Houston wrote Dr. Ashbel Smith, "The fuss is over and the sun yet shines as ever. What next?" After mentioning Thomas Rusk's recent suicide, he told Smith:

> I want to talk grave as well as laugh with you... Oh, I do want someone who has seen other days in Texas to talk with! ... If you come to see me, I bind myself to make you laugh.

Although sectional animosities were undiminished, in 1859, voters who were worried about Indian attack and Mexican border bandits had begun to realize that secession meant war. They wanted Houston's leadership. He made only one campaign speech, but Runnels never knew what hit him, as he lost by a margin of 27,500 to 36,227 votes.

Because of legislative hostility, Houston was inaugurated on the capitol's front portico. On December 21, 1859, declaring that secession was treason, he told a huge crowd,

> Half the care—half the thought—which had been spent in meeting sectionalism by sectionalism, and bitterness by bitterness, and abolitionism by disunion, would have made this people a happy, united and hopeful nation.

Samuel Maverick observed:

> What a blessing it is not to have Runnels here now, aggravating the mischief, as he did all the time he was Governor. Old Sam is the right man for this delicate occasion; for South Carolina would be fool enough to go out of the Union if only she had 3 or 4 states to go with her.

———

Friend, Lierena B., <u>Sam Houston, The Great Designer</u>, Austin: University of Texas Press, 1954.

James, Marquis, <u>The Raven</u>, Indianapolis: Bobbs-Merrill Company, 1929.

# THE TEXANS TURNED ON HOUSTON

After representatives from South Carolina, Mississippi, Alabama, Georgia, Florida and Louisiana met at Montgomery to form the Confederate States of America, Texas secessionists asked for a session of the legislature. Stating that Lincoln's election did not justify disunion, Governor Houston did not summon legislators until Oran Milo Roberts and others had launched the Secession Convention. Francis Lubbock explained Texas' situation in this fashion:

> As an original question, secession, perhaps, would have failed to carry in Texas; but six leading cotton states had already resorted to an exercise of the right, banded themselves together in a new confederation, and formed a new government. Texas was apparently confronted with the alternatives of becoming a party to the new compact, remaining in the Union, or resuming her sovereignty as a separate republic. Had she desired to desert her sister states of the South in this hour of need and peril (which she did not) and resume her former status as a republic, it was realized that she could not preserve a neutral attitude and maintain herself in that condition. The idea of remaining in the Union, and thereby arraying herself with the avowed enemies of the South, was not to be thought of. The course that was adopted was the only one that was open to her.

> Nor was she withheld from it by sentimental considerations. The Northern States generally sympathized with our Mexican enemies in our struggle

for independence and opposed our admission into the Union, Massachusetts going so far (by legislative resolution) as to declare the annexation of Texas, ipso facto, a dissolution of the Union. Our people really preferred to fight Massachusetts rather than Louisiana, if fighting should become necessary.

The Secession Convention met in Austin on January 28, 1861, and, by a vote of 166 to 7 adopted an ordinance dissolving the ties binding Texas to the United States. An election was called on the secession ordinance, and the convention recessed until March 2, the anniversary of Texas independence. When Houston refused to pledge fidelity to the Confederacy, he was replaced by Lieutenant Governor Edward Clark. Llerena Friend quoted William Baker on that time:

> As I look back into the darkness of those days, the central figure of them all is that of the old governor sitting in his chair in the basement of the capitol ... sorrowfully meditating what it were best to do.... The officers of the gathering upstairs summoned the old man three times to come forward and take the oath of allegiance ... to the Confederacy. I remember as yesterday the call thrice repeated — "Sam Houston! Sam Houston! Sam Houston!" But the man sat silent, immovable, in his chair below, whittling steadily on.

———

Friend, Llerena B., Sam Houston, The Great Designer, Austin: University of Texas Press, 1954.

Lubbock, Francis, Six Decades in Texas, Austin: Pemberton Press, 1968.

# A BRINDLE YEARLING ROAMED THE TRANS-PECOS COUNTRY

The Trans-Pecos country was lightly peopled in the last century. It is not exactly crowded now. As an opportunity to visit with neighbors, roundups were especially important.

In 1890, some cowmen staged a roundup near Alpine. The holiday spirit of those gatherings produced some horseplay, but seldom was there any trouble. Early in the proceedings, Fine Gilliland claimed a brindle yearling to which H. H. Powe (or Poe), a one-armed Confederate veteran, also asserted title.

Powe seemed to have the better claim, for the yearling was following a cow bearing Powe's brand. Even as their voices rose, most of the neighbors believed Gilliland and Powe were joking, and before anyone realized the gravity of the situation, pistols were drawn. The two men ran into the makeshift corral and were shooting over the backs of the frightened cattle.

A bullet struck Powe in the middle of the forehead, and he fell dead beneath the milling animals. Gilliland fled. Powe's son rode away to summon the Rangers, while the rest of the family took the body home.

The others returned to branding the calves, but the joy was gone from the occasion, and nothing could be done to restore their spirits. All that remained was to attend to the drudgery and go home.

Then, one of the men roped the brindle yearling. Others helped throw and hold him, and with a straight running iron, a cowhand burned a huge brand into the animal's side extending from shoulder to hip; it read "1890 MURDER."

The yearling was turned loose — was set free to roam that big, empty country. For half a century — for periods longer than anyone believed a steer could live — cowboys reported seeing the murder yearling. A rancher would tell about a hand who knew a mail carrier who spied the branded steer down by Marathon, or near Valentine, or Sanderson, or Marfa. As the years passed, the murder steer was reported to have been grazing outside Presidio, or close to Fort Davis, or Fort Stockton — a few times as far east as Midland County.

Now — a hundred years later — the last sighting of the brindle yearling may not yet have been made.

—

Casey, Clifford, <u>Mirages, Mysteries and Reality, Brewster County, Texas</u>, Seagraves: Pioneer Book Publishers, 1972.

# CLAY ALLISON NEVER KILLED A MAN WHO DID NOT NEED KILLING

Clay Allison was a legendary character, a gunfighter who inspired so many stories that now it is hard to separate fact from fiction. A Confederate veteran from Tennessee, Allison came to Texas after the war and made at least one cattle drive with Charles Goodnight before taking up residence in New Mexico.

Allison was as handy with a knife as he was with a pistol. One story had him dueling with Bowie knives in a freshly-dug grave — his left arm lashed to that of his opponent and the winner honor-bound to cover up the loser.

In another duel, the weapons of choice were Frontier Colts, and the setting was a dark ice house.

My favorite Allison tale appeared in The Tascosa Pioneer:

It is told of Clay Allison, who is getting well up in years but whose early habit of getting even with his enemies clings to him still was up in Cheyenne, Wyoming, when he had occasion to patronize a dentist. He had a bad tooth, and he wanted it pulled. The dentist was the merest quack, and he clumsily bored away at the wrong tooth and presently broke it off. This fired the cowman, and to get even he took that ignorant dentist up in no gentle grasp, floored him, seized his own forceps, and with a knee on his breast, amid the poor fellow's yells, jerked out one of his best teeth. Others would have followed, but friends came in and put a stop to it.

It was a tough but original way of having revenge.

Over his Pecos, Texas grave, a wooden marker is inscribed "Clay Allison, Gentleman Gun Fighter, 1840-1887, R. I. P.," and a headstone proclaims that, "He never killed a man that did not need killing."

—

The Tascosa Pioneer, July 24, 1886.

# DANIEL PARKER FOUNDED PILGRIM BAPTIST CHURCH

In 1832, Daniel Parker decided to found a primitive Baptist church in East Texas. Unable to do so, because the Roman Catholic Church was established by law, and no other denomination was permitted, Parker organized the Pilgrim Baptist Church in Illinois and led the thirty-six members to Elkhart, Anderson County, Texas.

Parker was the pastor of Pilgrim Church — perhaps the state's oldest Protestant congregation — until his death in 1844.

A delegate to the Consultation, Parker was elected to the House of Representatives of the Republic, although ministers were not eligible to serve. Eight other congregations were organized under the auspices of Pilgrim Church.

Pilgrim's rules provided for an investigation of the character of anyone absent "three meatings (sic) hand running." The minutes reflect that some members judged themselves harshly. Brother Mead confessed that he had been angry on election day, in 1850, and the minutes show that he was forgiven.

Brother Garrett declared himself beyond help and encouraged punitive action. He asked "the church to throw him overboard as was Jonah, so the church by her vote excluded Brother Garrett."

At least a dozen years before the Civil War began, slaves and freedmen were members of the congregation. In 1852, Quarley, a slave belonging to John Davis, was baptized, and, later, the church petitioned for Brother Quarley's freedom so that he could preach.

A replica of Pilgrim Baptist Church is maintained at Elkhart Cemetery, where many original settlers are buried.

—

De Shields, James T., <u>Cynthia Ann Parker</u>, St. Louis: Chas. B. Woodward Printing and Book Manufacturing Co., 1886.

"The Records of an Early Texas Baptist Church," <u>Quarterly of the Texas State Historical Association</u>, XII (July, 1908)

# CYNTHIA ANN WAS CAPTURED AT FORT PARKER

After Elder Daniel Parker brought the Pilgrim Baptist Church congregation to Anderson County, Texas, some of his kinsmen felt the need to move further west. In Limestone County, near present Mexia, in 1834, they established a private fort in which the cabins' outer walls formed part of a stockade. Loopholes for rifles and two elevated corner blockhouses made it possible for a few settlers to resist substantial Indian war parties. The families living at Fort Parker cultivated farms as far away as a mile.

The patriarch of the community was Elder John Parker, Elder Daniel's father. His sons, James, Silas, and Benjamin, and their families made up most of the fort's population of thirty-eight.

Fort Parker's people joined the Runaway Scrape—that stampede of terrified Texans, spurred by fears of Santa Anna's invading army, and fleeing eastward to the safety of the Sabine River's east bank. Learning of Houston's victory at San Jacinto on April 21, 1836 , the Fort Parker settlers returned home.

On May 19, 1836 — less than a month after the battle of San Jacinto -— a war party of 500 to 700 Comanche, Kiowa, and Indian allies stopped just outside rifle range of the fort. They raised a white flag, and Benjamin Parker went out to parley. The chief wanted directions to a spring.

Back inside the stockade, Benjamin told the others that the Indians were trying to determine how many men were present. In fact, James Parker, L. D. Nixon, Rachel Parker Plummer's husband, and four others were working their fields.

Silas Parker begged his brother to remain inside; the fort had been built for just such a situation. With the gate closed and the blockhouses manned, they could withstand an attack. But Benjamin went back to talk to the Indians. Rachel Plummer wrote,

> When Uncle Benjamin reached the body of Indians, they turned to the right and left and surrounded him.... I ran out of the fort, and passing the corner I saw the Indians drive their spears into Benjamin.

Instead of utilizing the fort for defense, the settlers did not even close the gate, and several ran outside the stockade. Silas Parker was killed. So were Samuel and Robert Frost, Elder John Parker, Granny Parker, Mrs. Duty, and Mrs. John Parker.

Rachel Plummer and her fifteen-month-old son, James Pratt Plummer, were captured. After a few days, they were separated when the war party split up. Mrs. Plummer never saw her child again.

Silas Parker's six-year-old son, John, and his daughter, Cynthia Ann, nine years old, were captured that morning, too. John was ransomed after several months, but Cynthia Ann lived twenty-four years with the Comanche and became the greatest of the Texas legends.

—

Haley, J. Evetts, <u>Charles Goodnight, Cowman and Plainsman</u>, Norman: University of Oklahoma Press, 1949.

Rister, Carl Coke, <u>Border Captives</u>, Norman: University of Oklahoma Press, 1940.

# CYNTHIA ANN PARKER SPENT A QUARTER CENTURY WITH THE COMANCHE

At age 18, Benjamin Franklin Gholson took part in an Indian fight on the Pease River. Afterward, the Rangers realized that a woman they had captured in the skirmish was white. She called herself "Palux" and the baby girl she carried "Curlin." Dried blood was caked in her hair and smeared over her face from buffalo they had been skinning.

Someone—perhaps Charles Goodnight—noticed her blue eyes and reddish hair and wondered whether she was the long-lost Cynthia Ann Parker, who had been carried away from Limestone County in 1836.

Colonel Isaac Parker was summoned to Fort Belknap in the hope that he could identify the Indian woman should she be, in fact, the child of his brother, Silas.

Gholson was present when Colonel Parker was shown into the tent where the woman was sitting on a pine box, holding the infant, whom historians usually call "Prairie Flower." He recalled that, "The wind was blowing cold from the north, and she was... on the south side of the tent, crouched low, with her elbows on her knees and her palms on her jaws."

Parker had said that he would be surprised if she remembered her original name, but when he stated. "I do know that my brother and his wife called her Cynthia Ann," the woman looked up and stared at him. Parker repeated the name, and then said it a third time. She arose, faced Parker, patted her chest, and said, "Me Cincee Ann!"

In this fashion was Cynthia Ann Parker identified, after spending almost a quarter century with the Comanche. As the wife of Peta Nocona, she had borne, in addition to the baby girl, two sons: Pecos, and Quanah, who would be the last war chief of the Quahadi Comanche.

—

Haley, J. Evetts, <u>Charles Goodnight, Cowman and Plainsman</u>, Norman: University of Oklahoma Press, 1949.

Rickard, J.A., <u>Brief Biographies of Brave Texans</u>, Dallas: Banks, Upshaw and Company, 1962.

Rister, Carl Coke, <u>Border Captives</u>, Norman: University of Oklahoma Press, 1940.

# GEORGE WEST'S OLD LONGHORN VISITED RUSSIA

Although longhorns were contrary beasts who made life difficult for those who worked with them, certain steers inspired a lasting affection in their owners. Charles Goodnight took special pride in Old Blue, a steer who led herds to market and returned to tasks on the JA Ranch requiring extraordinary strength and determination.

George West had such high regard for two longhorns that, when finally he leased his ranch, a pasture was set aside for them. One of those steers has occupied for many years a glass case on the Live Oak County courthouse square in the city of George West.

During the terrible drought of the 1880's, West was ranching 150,000 acres. The grass and water were nearly gone, and cattle were dying rapidly. To keep track of his losses, cowhands carried hatchets and brought in the left horn of each dead animal. Before the next rainfall, 2,200 horns were piled behind his house.

At the 1899 San Antonio International Fair, George West exhibited the best steer he had ever owned. A pure longhorn — sixteen years old and weighing 1,700 pounds — he was a lead steer, who like Goodnight's Blue, held the point as herds were walked to Kansas. J. Frank Dobie wrote:

> His horns had an upward curvature and when he stood at rest their tips were over eight feet above his hoofs. They measured seven feet and nine inches straight across and about nine feet following the curves.

That lead steer's companion is the mounted longhorn standing on the Live Oak County square. Dobie called it "a well-intentioned piece of work, but an execrable example of taxidermy." Two years old when George West bought him in Jackson County, he was twenty-two when a foot injury made it necessary that he be put down. A local writer claimed he weighed 2,200 pounds and had nine-foot, six-inch horns, but Dobie said they measured just over six feet. West's nephew hired a San Antonio taxidermist to mount the longhorn, and local businessmen built the glass case in 1927.

During the American Bicentennial, in 1976, Live Oak County citizens had the longhorn refurbished. Years of heat and insects and sunshine had left the old steer in poor condition. A new hide was obtained, and the extensive repairs and reconstruction cost almost $ 7,000. In a spasm of pride, someone decided that the Russians, having never seen a longhorn, were culturally deprived, so the steer— sometimes called Geronimo — became a popular exhibit on a Bicentennial train that toured the Soviet Union and other places the old longhorn had never thought of visiting.

—

Dobie, J. Frank, The Longhorns, New York: Bramhall House, 1961.
Haley, J. Evetts, Charles Goodnight, Cowman and Plainsman, Norman: University of Oklahoma Press, 1949.

# IMA WAS JIM HOGG'S ONLY DAUGHTER

Texans like a good story, and sometimes they are frustrated when truth gets in the way. A favorite tale concerns James Stephen Hogg, the first native-born governor—a huge, common man with a huge, common name. Candidates then delivered long speeches to large audiences. The need to be heard on the edges of a crowd, and the May heat, made it necessary that water be provided.

Once, Hogg shared the platform with a well-mannered opponent. A table held a wooden water bucket, a dipper, and two glasses. Hogg's opponent paused in his speech, dipped water from the bucket into a glass, and drank. He dabbed at his mouth with a freshly-starched handkerchief and returned to his argument. Everyone appreciated the candidate's style.

Hogg then belabored the railroads, banks, newspapers, and monopolies. He stopped, put down his notes, and while the shocked opponent watched, hoisted the bucket and drank from it. Water splashed onto his chest and puddled the platform. Spectators told about that performance for the rest of their days.

The best-known Jim Hogg story concerns the name he gave his daughter—Ima. Texans embellish the narrative by claiming that his other daughter was Eura Hogg. (Some, whose imaginations soar beyond any constraints of fact, tell of a third girl—Sheesa Hogg.)

In fact, Hogg fathered only four children: Tom, Will, Mike, and Ima. In choosing his daughter's name, he apparently failed to realize the consequences. (A man who wears an unusual name is seldom aware that it is uncommon.) Hogg believed he was simply honoring his deceased brother—a poet who had written about a girl named Ima.

Miss Ima Hogg never married. For 93 years, she wore that name without seeing any humor in it. Introducing herself, she would pause between her first and last names: "My name is Ima—Hogg."

Tell a Texan that there was no Eura Hogg, and he will protest. Explain the composition of the Hogg family, and he will argue some more. Should you convince him, he will not forgive you. Probably, you will have lost a friend, for Eura Hogg is precious to those who believe in her—in the same way the Easter Bunny, or Tooth Fairy, or Great Pumpkin hold special places in the hearts of devotees.

—

Iscoe, Louise Kosches, Ima Hogg, First Lady of Texas, Houston: The Hogg Foundation for Mental Health, 1976.

# JOSIAH WILBARGER LOST HIS HAIR

One day in August of 1833, Josiah Wilbarger and four others set out from Rueben Hornsby's home to survey land in present Travis County. At noon, they stopped about four miles east of present Austin to prepare a meal. Suddenly, they were attacked by Indians. Christian and Strother died immediately. Wilbarger was wounded in the hip, and arrows lodged in both legs. With no chance to unhobble his horse, Wilbarger tried to climb up behind Standifer. As he chased Standifer's horse, an Indian shot Wilbarger through the neck, and he fell — apparently dead.

Standifer and Haynie hurried to warn those staying at Hornsby's place. Having seen the Indians scalp him and take his clothes, they reported that Wilbarger was dead.

That night, Mrs. Hornsby awoke her husband. In a dream, she had seen Wilbarger. A woman had led her to a tree where Wilbarger sat with his back against the trunk. Mrs. Hornsby insisted that Wilbarger was still alive, but Hornsby told her to go back to sleep. Later, she roused him once more. Having had the same dream again, she was more certain than before that Wilbarger lived and hoped to be rescued. In order to pacify her, Hornsby promised to lead a search party at daylight.

Reaching the scene of the massacre, Hornsby's company found Wilbarger beneath a tree. He was naked, badly injured, covered with blood, and without his scalp. Fearing that the rescuers might mistake him for an Indian because of his sunburn and the blood smeared over his body, the wounded man yelled, "Don't shoot, it is Wilbarger."

Wilbarger stated that during the night his sister, who lived in

Missouri, had appeared in a dream and promised him that help was coming. Then she walked away in the direction of Hornsby's place.

A few weeks later, Wilbarger learned that his sister had died on the night he spent at the scene of the massacre. He lived eleven years without his hair and died after accidently bumping his head on a low rafter in his barn.

Wilbarger's son, John, was killed by Indians while on Ranger service in 1850. Wilbarger County — Vernon is the seat of government — honors Josiah and his brother, Mathias.

—

Wilbarger, J. W., Indian Depredations in Texas, Austin: The Steck Company, 1935.

# CARPETBAG JUDGES
# GENERATED LITTLE RESPECT

---

Reconstruction was a difficult time in Texas. Former governor Francis Lubbock's attitude was not untypical. He stated,

> I am not disposed to write of the times when Texas was writhing under the heel of military despotism and vultures were preying upon her vitals.... Venality and tyranny were rampant, all the safeguards of liberty were overthrown....

Texans deeply resented the carpetbagger judges appointed by E. J. Davis, the Reconstruction governor. Captain William J. Strong described the treatment accorded a district judge — who only recently had been a shoemaker — in the first term of court held in Brownwood after the war.

Responding to spectator comments upon his obvious lack of qualifications, the new judge said, "Now men, let's go on with court, let's go on with court. Now, we must go on with this court."

At Weatherford, pranksters penned a bull yearling inside the courtroom on the evening before the term was to begin, and that temple of justice sustained heavy damage.

In Erath County, John Morrison, of Dublin, decorated a burro with ribbons while a fiddler entertained the spectators. Morrison nearly exhausted Frey Brothers' inventory as he tied a ribbon every place that would support one.

Then, seizing the burro's ears, Morrison and a friend followed the fiddler into the house where the shoemaker-judge was presiding. The fiddler stepped aside as the burro entered the crowded courtroom.

The judge yelled, "Mr. Sheriff, fine each of them thar men ten dollars and hold 'em until it's paid."

Morrison threw a twenty dollar coin and a ten dollar gold piece to the floor, ordered, "Right about, march!" and, to the strains of the fiddle music, led the procession out of the courtroom.

—

Lubbock, Francis, <u>Six Decades in Texas</u>, Austin: Pemberton Press, 1968.
Strong, Henry W., <u>My Frontier Days and Indian Fights</u>.

# TEXAS WAS A REMOTE HINTERLAND

For most of the last century, Texas was so remote and isolated that settlers might reasonably fear they would never again see relatives in the old states. Richard Hamilton Hill, of Walnut Creek, Bastrop County, expressed that concern in this October 5, 1868 letter to Kentucky:

Well my dear brother Franklin:

As my entire family have all gone to church leaving me home to keep house I have determined that this day I will write you a letter ....

I am now in the enjoyment of good health having undergone no change that I am sensible of except my eyesight and elasticity of limbs have failed me some, the former considerable ....

My wife is now looking old; older than I do. She has not enjoyed all together as good health as I have, consequently is more broken than I am. We have had twelve children, six boys and six girls.... All stout, healthy and vigorous, and, so far as I am allowed to judge, possessing a fair portion of intellect; all from Walter up are pretty well educated considering the many obstacles in Texas that are in the way of conducting schools properly and successfully.

When I came to Texas I commenced with 100 head of cattle and 40 mares and 150 hogs. Pretty much all have been stolen. So that I quit the stock business entirely and am ... farming all together for a living....

We often talk of you all and as often wish we could enjoy the society of your country. This is only musing for we are never to enjoy so great a happiness this side of the grave. And as the separation has been from childhood to old age, the bare recollection almost of names has become obliterated and scarcely a dream remains to remind us of the days of our greatest happiness when all were sheltered under one roof the home of Pa and Ma. All older and many younger than I have exited to eternity, and I, too, ere long must be of that number.

—

Donnelly, Sister Mary Louise, <u>Genealogy of Thomas Hill and Rebecca Miles</u>, 1971.

# FUEL WAS SCARCE IN
# DALLAM COUNTY

Dallam County is situated in the northwest corner of the Texas Panhandle. The seat of government, Dalhart, straddles the boundary separating Dallam and Hartley counties.

Dallam's first capital, Texline, was the subject of this 1888 Tascosa Pioneer story:

> Texline has been decided upon as the end of a passenger and freight division on this road, and will be built up by a combined effort of the railroad company and the XIT interests, and there is a prevalent opinion that as it is right at the line of Texas and New Mexico, close to No Man's Land and not far from the corners of Kansas and Colorado, it will be the biggest and the best and the fastest and the hardest and the busiest and the wildest and the roughest and the toughest town of this section. They've already had to station the Texas Rangers there — and when that's said enough's said.

Fuel was a critical problem in that treeless country. Families regularly spent entire days picking up coal that had fallen from trains passing over the Fort Worth and Denver track, and sometimes they pilfered railroad coal bins. Men came to Texline from forty miles around to buy coal from the railroad — the only commercial source of supply.

The Fort Worth and Denver Railway Company considered the small transactions a nuisance. Attempting to discourage customers, the railroad did not provide scales. The quantity of coal purchased had to be estimated each time, usually to the advantage of the railroad.

Lillie Hunter told of a poor farmer who arrived after the station agent had gone home for the night. Having come a long distance, and unable to neglect his farm and family to make another trip, the nester tried to serve himself. He drove under the coal chute and opened the trap. The wagon filled quickly, but the farmer could not shut off the flow. A mountain of coal crushed his wagon and spread onto the tracks. Mrs. Hunter wrote:

> The man took his team and left the wagon there. No one ever knew who it was nor did they try to find out. The section crew was called out to clear the main track of the railroad as they couldn't get any trains through.

—

Hunter, Lillie, The Book of Years, Hereford: Pioneer Book Publishers, 1969.
Tascosa Pioneer, October 20, 1888.

# DANCING WAS IMPORTANT IN THE REPUBLIC

Early Texians were serious about their dancing, and they made the most of the limited opportunities.

The New Orleans Picayune told of an army captain who came upon dancers in the Republic trying to revive a drunken fiddler. The only musician in the county, he had imbibed to excess and passed out, creating a desperate situation.

While the captain may have taken some liberties with the truth, generally he was trustworthy. He reported that the dancers rolled the fiddler on the floor, rubbed his head with vinegar, and "crammed an entire jar of Underwood's pickles down his throat." The inebriate did not respond to any of those traditional remedies.

Although the captain had never before held a fiddle, he stepped onto the stage and — acting as if he knew what he was doing — gave the strings a "general rake with the bow." The grateful dancers reacted with enthusiasm,

> Away they went like mad, Captain H. still sawing away, stamping his right foot as if keeping time.... It may be supposed that the dancers had but a limited knowledge of music; but still they could tell, in their cooler moments, a tune from a tornado.

All went reasonably well for a few sets. Then a man asked his partner, "Eliza, did you ever hear that tune he's aplaying afore?"

"Can't say that I ever has."

Even though the captain overheard the conversation, he kept

belaboring the fiddle.

"Does it sound to you like much of a tune?"

"Well, it doesn't."

"Nor to me either," said the man, struggling to discover a melody. "My opinion is that that feller there is naterally jest promiscuously and miscellaneously sawin away without exactly knowing what he's a doin."

—

Hogan, William Ransom, The Texas Republic, Austin: University of Texas Press, 1969.

# SAM WOODY WAS WISE COUNTY'S ORIGINAL SETTLER

Wise County's first permanent settler, Sam Woody, built his log cabin in 1854, two years before sufficient population existed to organize a local government. (By 1867, there were only 400 residents, and Indians were still a problem; a Comanche war party killed Nicholas Dawson in 1870.)

Woody, a well-beloved citizen, left this account of pioneering in North Texas:

> It was easy to live in those days. Sow five or six acres of wheat, it would often produce fifty bushels to the acre, cut it with a cradle, tramp and fan it out, then once or twice a year load up a wagon to which five or six steers were hitched, and after a week's trip to Dallas you would have enough flour to give bread to your family and some of the neighbors for a number of weeks, until it would be the turn of someone else to make the trip.

> If we had bread enough, game was always plentiful. Hogs would get so fat on acorns that they couldn't walk. After marking them we let them run wild, and trained our dogs to run them in whenever we wanted a supply of pork. Now and then we sent a wagon to Shreveport or Houston for coffee and sugar and such groceries, but we did not use sugar much. I paid a dollar for a pint of the first sorghum seed planted in Wise County, and molasses was the commonest kind of "sweetening." When we got tired of game and pork

we killed a beef. By swinging a quarter high up to the limb of a tree it would be safe from wild animals and would keep sweet for weeks, and it was a common sight in our country to see the woman of the house untying the rope and letting down the meat to cut off enough for dinner.

At an old settlers reunion, the master of ceremonies acknowledged Woody's presence with the comment that local civilization dated from the time he came down out of the trees.

—

Wise County Historical Commission, <u>Wise County History</u>, Volume II, Decatur: 1982.

# EAST DALLAS RESEMBLED A SMALL TOWN IN WORLD WAR II

To anyone growing up in Gainesville during the Depression, Dallas was the great city of Texas. We did not imagine that, in many ways, "Big D" — or "Big Friendly" — was then only an assemblage of communities. I learned that from a tape made by Mrs. Ruth Collins, who said, "I loved East Texas when I was a girl. And I loved East Dallas."

In World War II, Dallas was — perhaps — just Gainesville writ large. The only air conditioning systems belonged to cafes and theaters with signs promising "20 degrees cooler" interiors. Families spent time outdoors. In the evenings, they visited neighbors and kinfolk and sat on front porches while children "played out." They chased fireflies and scuffled and the evening would conclude with parents calling their children to come in — it was bedtime. Each child understood the unwritten and unspoken rule against responding or obeying until a parent's tone was appropriately menacing.

Mrs. Collins claimed that East Dallas had the "top corner drugstore of the world," where young people could sprawl on the floor, read comic books from the racks, and perhaps buy a nickel Coke in the course of an afternoon.

Wondering where her son had gone after classes let out at Woodrow Wilson High, a mother could call the druggist, who would report the last sighting of the young fellow or summon him to the phone if he could break away from his comic book.

Mrs. Collins said, "We wouldn't have thought about raising our children without the help of that good man."

Her sons joined the Army in World War II, and she wrote them every day. Should she run out of stamps, Mrs. Collins could order a roll of three centers charged to her account and delivered to her home. There was no profit in selling stamps, and the delivery and extension of credit were simply expenses the merchant incurred for his customers' convenience.

When boys the druggist had hosted entered the armed forces, their parents brought photographs in new uniforms, and the merchant displayed them in a huge frame. He never realized how much the people of East Dallas loved him, Mrs. Collins believed. And when his Navy pilot son was lost at sea, he could not have known how deeply the loss was felt by hundreds of people he had never met.

—

# MARCY BELIEVED THE PLAINS COULD NEVER BE SETTLED

Probably no man played a more important part in the early settlement of Northwest Texas than Randolph Barnes Marcy, a West Pointer and veteran of the Mexican War battles of Palo Alto and Resaca de La Palma.

In 1849, Marcy was ordered to escort from Fort Smith, Arkansas, to Santa Fe, New Mexico, 2,000 immigrants who were bound for California because of the gold discovered at Sutters Fort. Marcy was to locate and mark a good route for the hordes who would join the gold rush.

In describing the Staked Plains, Marcy noted that the ground west of the Upper Cross Timbers was "as smooth and firm as a macadamized road almost the entire distance to Santa Fe." Arriving on the Caprock, Marcy wrote:

> When we were upon the high table-land, a view presented itself as boundless as the ocean. Not a tree, shrub, or any other object, either animate or inanimate, relieved the dreary monotony of the prospect; it was a vast illimitable expanse of desert prairie — the dreaded "Llano Estacado" of New Mexico; or, in other words, the great Zahara of North America. It is a region almost as vast and trackless as the ocean — a land where no man, either savage or civilized, permanently abides; it spreads north into a treeless, desolate waste of uninhabited solitudes, which always has been and must continue, uninhabited forever; even the savages dare not venture to cross it except at two or three

places, where they know water can be found. The only herbage upon these barren plains is a very short buffalo grass.

To the east, the country was well-suited for cultivation, but the Plains were:

> ... an ocean of barren prairie, with but here and there a feeble stream and a few solitary trees. It would seem as if the Creator had designed this as an immense natural barrier beyond which agriculturalists should not pass, leaving the great prairies for the savage to roam at will.

Marcy returned to civilization over a more southern route; that trail became the main east-west thoroughfare — California Street—in Gainesville, one of the towns that drew settlers from the stream of gold seekers.

—

Marcy, Randolph Barnes, <u>Exploration of the Red River of Louisiana in the Year 1852</u>.

# ELLEN OWENS REMEMBERED THE INDIAN TERRITORY

My grandmother, Ellen Owens, was born in Wise County well over a century ago. She married Tom Prigmore, and they homesteaded in the Indian Territory. Once, she told me about Tom's habit of coming in from the fields in the evening singing as loudly as he could, "Oh, my pretty Ellie."

While plowing one day, Tom suffered a stroke, fell face down and suffocated in the soft earth of the furrow. My grandmother was left with four children below the age of six. Since the well on the place was gyppy, drinking water had to be hauled in.

Ellen Owens Prigmore then married Jim Prigmore, Tom's younger brother, and my mother was the only child of that union.

When my grandmother was ninety-five years old and living in Anderson, California, I asked, "How did you make it?"

She said — and she wasn't trying to be funny — "I don't know."

My grandmother played the guitar and sang thirty verses from "The Ballad of Sam Bass." She recited poems for me that she had learned as a child in Wise County, and she told about her first proposal of marriage. He was a scholar at the Decatur Baptist College and was studying to be an "exhorter." He dropped to one knee and recited from the Book of Ruth, "Entreat me not to leave thee, for whither thou goest I will go, and whither thou lodgest I will lodge, thy people shall be my people, and thy God my God."

"It was magnificent," my grandmother said. "I wish you

could have been there." She savored the memory, then added,

> I told my neighbor about that the other day, and she just
> sat with her mouth open. She said, "Ellie, if I had ever
> had a man feel that way about me, I would have swum
> Tar River for him."

Just about a year before our conversation, the City of Anderson trimmed some trees and left the branches at the curb to be hauled away. My grandmother said, "I looked at those limbs for near onto a week. I would think how cornbread used to taste baked in the open over a wood fire in Greer County, in the Indian Territory."

Finally, unable to stand it longer, with her hatchet — dull from age and lack of use — she chopped enough wood for the fire she built on the sidewalk. Then — with batter prepared from long ago memory — she baked some cornbread that she claimed tasted exactly as it had so long ago in the Indian Territory.

—

# AN ARMY DOG GREW OLD IN THE SERVICE OF HIS COUNTRY

Sergeant H. H. McConnell came to Texas with the United States Army's Sixth Cavalry Regiment soon after the end of the Civil War. He owned and operated McConnell's Drug Store, at Jacksboro.

When, in his old age, McConnell published his memoir of military life, he recalled with affection the army's dogs, and, in particular, "Old Taylor," a large, shaggy, powerful, "yaller" hound who had "joined" at Buffalo Springs, moved on to Fort Richardson, and finally trudged 700 miles to Kansas. McConnell wrote:

> One of the soldier's predilections is his love for dogs, and his propensity for them was such that every detail returning from the settlements was accompanied by a new lot of curs that they had induced to come with them. Our regiment was always overrun with dogs-
>
> "Mongrel, puppy, whelp, and hound, And curs of low degree,"
>
> Some valuable greyhounds among them, but mostly of the "yaller dog" species.
>
> At the sound of the bugle every dog would set up a howl, until at times the nuisance would become epidemic, as it were, and a special order be issued to exterminate all those running loose on the parade ground.
>
> Our company had a big, hairy, nondescript dog that

"joined" at Jacksboro in 1868, and attached himself to the guard-house, and nothing could induce him to visit other parts of the garrison, except when he sometimes accompanied the guard on its rounds. The guards and prisoners shared their food with him; he tramped along with the guard to Kansas when the regiment was moved there in 1871, and I last saw him at Fort Hays in the fall of that year, growing old "in the service" [of his country].

Old sergeant McConnell closed with this salute:

All honor to old Taylor! Unlike his superior animal, man, he stuck right loyally to his friends in adversity and seemed proud of the companionship.

—

McConnell, H. H., Five Years A Cavalryman, Jacksboro: J. N. Rogers & Company, 1889, pp. 132, 199, 200.

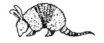

# TOM O'LOUGHLIN WAS THE ORIGINAL PANHANDLE SETTLER

Charles Goodnight, trail driver, plainsman, and builder of the JA Ranch, is usually considered the founding father of the Texas Panhandle; however, the first settler was probably Thomas O'Loughlin.

Buffalo hunter O'Loughlin accompanied troops who were sent to keep the Plains Indians from abandoning the reservations and returning to their old hunting grounds. Because the Comanche still were drawn to the Panhandle, where buffalo continued to be plentiful, the Army established Fort Elliott in present Wheeler County, Texas, on the western edge of the Indian Territory — present Oklahoma.

An early Mobeetie settler described a passing herd of some three million buffalo:

> From a high ridge near Fort Elliott I could see the herd for five or six miles in every direction. They were roaming northward and for three days you could not tell that they had moved.

O'Loughlin built the first house in Mobeetie, the town that grew up near Fort Elliot. His wife began taking in boarders, and as her business increased and the buffalo herds dwindled, O'Loughlin gave up hunting to help her. Later, he operated Mobeetie's Grand Central Hotel.

In 1876, when Charles Goodnight decided to move to the Panhandle, he boarded with O'Loughlin, who then guided Goodnight's cowboys and herd from the Canadian River to Palo

Duro Canyon.

In its prime, Mobeetie had thirteen saloons and a dance hall. Postmaster George Montgomery recalled that there also was a restaurant

> ... run by Tom O'Laughlin and wife, Helen, who was the only virtuous woman in town. There were [in Mobeetie] about fifteen dance hall girls ... bullwhackers, mule skinners, buffalo hunters and gamblers galore.

—

Porter, Millie Jones, <u>Memory Cups of Panhandle Pioneers</u>, Clarendon: Clarendon Press, 1945.

# WAGON FREIGHTERS WERE A BREED APART

Before the arrival of the railroad and the advent of trucks, Texas freight was hauled in wagons drawn by mules and oxen. The freighters were a special breed. Brownwood groceryman C. Y. Early wrote of one of them:

> He could neither read nor write.... He wanted to find a widow who could read and write if the learning did not make her so "stuck-up " that she would not milk and cook. One of the warehouse boys directed him to the home of a lady he felt might be interested. The old fellow went "a-courtin of this widow" on one of these trips, but he got no further than the front porch. The widow preferred to remain in bereavement rather than attempt to meet the requirements he exacted.

Oklahoma governor "Alfalfa Bill" Murray (who was born in Grayson County, Texas, and grew up in Parker County) left this account of his father's technique for harnessing five pairs of oxen:

> He would call the "wheelers," the yoke that worked on the tongue; the steer on the right side, he would lay the yoke over his neck, calling him to his place, slip the bow up and insert the key; back up and hold at arm's length the other end of the yoke; and call the (other) steer to walk under, and then in like manner the next yoke, until the five were "yoked up." Then a long chain with links half an inch thick or more ran back to the axle, with a hook to catch in the ring in the center of each yoke; then he was ready to go.

After the five yoke, or pairs, were hooked-up, my father began to sing off the names of the ten oxen by pairs. As the names of each pair (yoke) was called, beginning with the "Leaders," or front yoke, they would step up to get the chain taut, and weave back and forth till all yokes were called to the last yoke, the "Wheelers" that were on the tongue; and the chain taut to the end.

Murray's method suggests something of techniques Clement Moore must have known as he imagined how to drive reindeer in The Night Before Christmas.

His "song" would be: "Tom and Jerry, Tobe and Toney, Black and Brindle, Jim and Rector, Rock and Lion." Then cracking his whip in the air over their backs he cried out: "Come out of there!" The wagon began to move.... To my child-mind, this was a wonderful sight. I learned to call off the names of the five yokes, as he did.

—

Early, C. Y., Walker-Smith Company, Wholesale Grocers, 1894-1944, Dallas: 1944.

Murray, William, Memoirs of Governor Murray and True History of Oklahoma, Boston: Meador Publishing Company, 1945.

# LIZZIE CAMPBELL INTENDED TO LIVE A DIGNIFIED LIFE

The Texas Panhandle was always a difficult place. In 1542, it was Coronado's chronicler who was depressed by the vastness and emptiness of the Plains. Later, a cowboy would cease talking and retreat into himself, oppressed by the sameness of the terrain in every direction, and a friend would explain, "He's got the loneliness," which — being translated — meant that he had been overwhelmed by the monotonous, flat country, the absence of trees, and the constantly blowing wind.

The Plains were especially hard on women. The old saw was, "It's fine country for men and mules, but it's hell on horses and women. "

When Charles Goodnight moved to a dugout on the floor of the Palo Duro Canyon, his wife's nearest neighbor was seventy-five miles away and the closest town two hundred miles distant. Goodnight's biographer, J. Evetts Haley, wrote:

> The solitude and the wind were trying for a woman, and it was quite a domestic blessing when one day a cowboy rode in with three chickens in a sack. "No one can ever know how much pleasure and company they were to me," Mrs. Goodnight once said. "They were something I could talk to. They would run to me when I called them and follow me everywhere I went. They knew me and tried to talk to me in their language."

The women of the Plains maintained their standards, although the raw country sometimes modified their aspirations. Laura Hamner wrote of a young woman, recently arrived, who complained to ladies at a Sunday afternoon social that in Virginia she had never washed out so much as a pocket handkerchief. A lady who had been there longer than the others said quietly, "There wasn't none of us that were washerwomen before we come to this country."

Like the others, Lizzie Campbell insisted upon living at a certain level. She persuaded her husband — the manager of the Matador Ranch — to paint their house white, and she wore starched white dresses in that realm of dust storms that filled the sky with red dirt and invaded every corner of the best-kept home.

Mrs. Campbell said, "I mean to live a dignified life."

—

Haley, J. Evetts, <u>Charles Goodnight, Cowman and Plainsman</u>, Norman: University of Oklahoma Press, 1949.

Hamner, <u>Laura, Light n' Hitch</u>, Dallas: American Guild Press, 1958.

# GOD WILLING, MULKEY WOULD EXERCISE RESTRAINT

Old Texans loved to argue religion and hear the Bible debated. A Methodist circuit rider would meet a Baptist preacher in a struggle that might fill four hours on each of two or three nights, and the church would be packed to the rafters. A follower of Alexander Campbell might debate a Presbyterian, or two ministers of the same denomination would go to the mat over specific points of doctrine and practice.

At Comanche, the Methodist Peter Gravis was scheduled to confront a formidable Baptist, "Choctaw Bill." In preparation, Gravis rode to Stephenville to study books he hoped would support his position.

After "Choctaw Bill" refused to meet Gravis, J. M. Johnson stepped in as Gravis' replacement. In the six-day debate which followed, "Choctaw Bill" was vanquished. Gravis wrote, "His church scattered and was for years without a pastor."

—

Methodist minister Andrew Hunter told of a conversation with the great William Mulkey on the subject of forebearance. What was the duty of the Christian? How much imposition must the good man suffer from the wicked without retaliating? Hunter wrote,

> I remember asking him the question direct: "Brother Mulkey, suppose a wicked fellow should come up to you and say, 'Brother Mulkey, I am going to whip you.' What would you do?" To which Mulkey replied,

"I would say to him, 'Sir, if the Lord gives me grace,
I will bear it; but if not, woe be to your hide.'"

—

Gravis, Peter, <u>Twenty-Five Years on the Outside Row</u>, Brownwood: Cross Timbers Press, 1966, pp. 34, 38, 39.

Phelan, Macum, <u>A History of Early Methodism in Texas, 1817-1866</u>, Dallas: Cokesbury Press, 1924, pp. 185-6.

# POTTER WAS THE FIGHTING PARSON

---

Missouri-born Andrew Jackson Potter became — as the Reverend H. A. Graves put it — "the recognized wit of the grogshops of Bastrop, Texas, where he was, in 1856, converted."

As a Methodist minister, Potter rode a frontier circuit where the threat of hostile Indians and badmen made it necessary that he go armed. He wore a .45 Colt and carried a Winchester rifle.

Potter sometimes held religious services in the Kimble County courthouse at Junction. Placing his Bible, pistol, and rifle on the table beside him, he would announce, "Now, by the grace of God, and with the help of these, I will preach."

One Sunday, Potter arrived at a Caldwell County schoolhouse where he was to preach and found a crowd of toughs waiting for him. The leader of the thugs announced that horseraces would begin at eleven. He freely admitted that the contests had been scheduled after Potter's services were set for that hour.

Potter then stated that worship services would begin on time. The door would remain open so he could see into the yard from the pulpit. The first man who galloped past would find himself the owner of at least one brand new bullet hole. That solved the problem. The gang came inside to listen to Potter's sermon.

When he preached in Kimble County, Potter stayed with the father of future governor Coke Stevenson. On his last visit, Potter stated, "Bob, I think the Lord has too many preachers down here. He's calling too many of us home."

On October 31, 1895, he preached at Tilman Chapel, near Lockhart. After the closing prayer, Potter said, "Now I think you have heard my last sermon." He asked that the collection for the conference be brought forward quickly, and then — as Allie Loeffler put it — he "fell down and died, in the pulpit, without a struggle."

—

The Junction Eagle, June 10, 1976

# CLARENDON'S FIRST CHURCH STANDS IN DALHART

The third-oldest town in the Panhandle, Clarendon, was founded by Methodist minister L. H. Carhart and Godly folk who insisted that strong drink be prohibited in their county. Cowhands, and many other residents of the Plains, considered the situation an outrage and viewed Clarendon with disdain.

A judge in Mobeetie or Tascosa once sentenced a defendant to a week in Clarendon as the best substitute for solitary confinement available in the Panhandle.

A benefactor offered Clarendon's Methodist congregation a 500-pound bell that had won a prize at Philadelphia's centennial celebration if the Texans would pay the shipping costs. The bell came by railroad to Dodge City, Kansas, and by ox wagon to the Panhandle. The freight charges were $250.

After the Fort Worth and Denver tracks missed Clarendon, the town was moved five miles to the right-of-way, but the church and bell were abandoned at their original location. Methodists in Dalhart learned of the situation and asked if they might have the building to house their congregation. Carhart readily consented, and men from Dalhart rode down to Clarendon, dismantled the church, and hauled it, the bell, and the organ to the railroad for transport to Dallam County.

As news of the transaction spread, Clarendon residents — who had shown no particular interest in the discarded building — were suddenly concerned and furious. A mob, now passionately attached to the church house and bell, gathered to halt the removal, but the Dalhart Methodists drew six-shooters and held the grumbling Clarendon protestors at bay until the train was loaded and ready to depart. Lillie Hunter observed that, "In this dramatic manner one of the youngest towns in the Panhandle became home to the oldest church on the Plains."

In time, the building was acquired by Dalhart's Assembly of God, "but the historic bell was installed in the new (Methodist) bell tower where its silver notes still sprinkle the Sunday morning air with blessing."

—

Hunter, Lillie, <u>The Book of Years</u>, Hereford: Pioneer Book Publishers, 1969.

## REFERENCES

### Books

Andrus, Pearl, Juana, Waco: 1982.

Anon, Life and Adventures of Sam Bass, the Notorious Union Pacific and Texas Train Robber, Dallas: Dallas Commercial Steam Printing, 1878.

Bridges, C. A., A History of Denton County, Texas, 1978.

Brown, John Henry, History of Texas, 1685-1892, St. Louis: L. E. Daniell, 1893.

Brown, Ray Hyer, Robert Stewart Hyer, The Man I Knew, Salado: Anson Jones Press, 1957.

Chrysler, Walter P., Life of an American Workman, New York: Dodd, Mead, 1937.

Clark, Pat, Clarksville and Old Red River County, Dallas: Mathis, Van Nort & Company, 1937.

Clark, Randolph, Reminiscences, Fort Worth: Texas Christian University Press, 1979.

Clarke, Mary Whatley, David G. Burnet, Austin: Pemberton Press, 1969.

Dawson, Joseph, Jose Antonio Navarro, Waco: Baylor University Press, 1969.

De Cordova, Jacob, Texas: Her Resources and Her Public Men, Philadelphia: J. B. Lippincott, 1858.

De Shields, James P., They Sat In High Place, San Antonio: Naylor Publishers, 1940.

Dewees, W. B., Letters From an Early Settler of Texas, Louisville, Kentucky: Morton and Griswold, 1852.

Dobie, J. Frank, The Longhorns, New York: Bramhall House, 1961.

Donnelly, Sister Mary Louise, <u>Genealogy of Thomas Hill and Rebecca Miles</u>, 1971.

Eaves, Charles, and Hutchinson, C. A., <u>Post City, Texas</u>, Austin: The Texas State Historical Association, 1952.

Ewell, Thomas T., <u>A History of Hood County, Texas</u>, Granbury: 1895.

Frantz, Joe B., <u>Gail Borden, Dairyman to a Nation</u>, Norman: University of Oklahoma Press, 1951.

Gambrell, Herbert, <u>Anson Jones, The Last President of Texas</u>, Austin: University of Texas Press, 1964.

Glines, Carroll V., <u>Jimmy Doolittle, Daredevil Aviator and Scientist</u>, New York: Macmillan & Company, 1972.

Gracy, David B. II, <u>Moses Austin: His Life</u>, San Antonio: Trinity University Press, 1987.

Granbury Junior Woman's Club, <u>Hood County in Picture and Story</u>, Fort Worth: Historical Publications, 1978.

Gravis, Peter, <u>Twenty-Five Years on the Outside Row</u>, Brownwood: Cross Timbers Press, 1966.

Haley, J. Evetts, <u>Charles Goodnight, Cowman and Plainsman</u>, Norman: University of Oklahoma Press, 1949.

Hall, Helen and Hall, Roy, <u>Collin County</u>, Quanah: Nortex Press, 1975.

Hamner, Laura, <u>Light n' Hitch</u>, Dallas: American Guild Press, 1958.

Hay, Kenneth, <u>Life and Influence of Charles Carlton</u>, Fort Worth: 1940.

Johnson, Carrie, <u>A History of Young County, Texas</u>, Austin: Texas State Historical Association, 1956.

Johnson, Frank W., <u>A History of Texas and Texans</u>, Eugene Barker, ed., Chicago: American Historical Society, 1914.

Jones, Anson, Republic of Texas, Its History and Annexation, Chicago: Rio Grande Press, 1966.

Kendall, George Wilkins, Narrative of the Texas Santa Fe Expedition, Washington, D. C.: 1850.

Kittrell, N. G., Governors Who Have Been and Other Public Men, Houston: Dealy-Adey-Elgin Company, 1921.

Lindbergh, Charles A., The Spirit of St. Louis, New York: Scribners, 1952.

Lindbergh, Charles A., We, New York: Putnam, 1927.

Landrum, Graham and Smith, Allan, Grayson County, Fort Worth: Historical Publishers, 1967.

Lubbock, Francis, Six Decades in Texas, Austin: Pemberton Press, 1968.

Lucas, Mattie and Hall, Mita, A History of Grayson County, Sherman: Scruggs Printing Company, 1936.

McConnell, H. H., Five Years A Cavalryman, Jacksboro: J. N. Rogers & Company, 1889.

Moore, Jerome, Texas Christian University: A Hundred Years of History, Fort Worth: Texas Christian University Press, 1974.

Murphy, James. B., L. Q. C. Lamar: Pragmatic Patriot, Baton Rouge: Louisiana State University Press, 1973.

Nation, Carry A., The Use and Need of the Life of Carry A. Nation, Topeka: Steves, 1904.

Olmsted, Frederick Law, A Journey Through Texas, Austin: University of Texas Press, 1978.

Phelan, Macum, A History of Early Methodism in Texas, 1817-1866, Dallas: Cokesbury Press, 1924.

Porter, Millie Jones, Memory Cups of Panhandle Pioneers, Clarendon: Clarendon Press, 1945.

Rickenbacker, Edward V., Rickenbacker, Englewood Cliffs, N.J.: Prentice-Hall, Inc., 1967.

Smith, A. Morton, The First 100 Years in Cooke County, San Antonio: The Naylor Company, 1955.

Smithwick, Noah, The Evolution of a State, Austin: Steck-Vaughn Company, 1968.

Sterling, William Warren, Trails and Trials of a Texas Ranger, Norman: University of Oklahoma Press, 1968.

Taylor, T. U., Fifty Years on Forty Acres, Austin: Alec Book Company, 1938.

Thomas, Mary Martha, Southern Methodist University, Dallas: Southern Methodist University Press, 1974.

Wise County Historical Commission, Wise County History, Volume II, Decatur: 1982.

Wofford, Vera, Hale County, Facts and Folklore, Lubbock: Pica Publishing Company, 1978.

Young County Historical Survey Committee, Graham Centennial History: 1872-1972, Graham: 1972.

Zuber, William, My Eighty Years in Texas, Austin: University of Texas Press, 1971.

## Theses

Armstrong, James, "The History of Harrison County, Texas, 1839-1880," M. A. thesis, University of Colorado, 1930.

Greer, Joubert Lee, "The Building of the Texas State Capitol: 1882-1888," M. A. thesis, University of Texas at Austin, 1932.

Hinton, William, "A History of Howard Payne College with Emphasis on the Life and Administration of Thomas H. Taylor," Ed. D. dissertation, University of Texas at Austin, 1956.

Hitt, Bowling, "History of Howard Payne College," M. A. thesis, Sul Ross State University, 1951.

McDonald, Johnnie, "The Soldiers of San Jacinto," M. A. thesis, University of Texas at Austin, 1922.

Marshall, Elmer Grady, "The History of Brazos County, Texas," M. A. thesis, University of Texas at Austin, 1937.

Sloan, Sallie Everett, "The Presidential Administration of David G. Burnet, March 17 - October 22, 1836, With a Sketch of His Career," M. A. thesis, University of Texas at Austin, 1918.

Wilcox, Lois, "The Early History of Bryan," M. A. thesis, University of Texas at Austin, 1952.

### Journals, Magazines, Newspapers

Crume, Paul, The Dallas Morning News, December 25, 1958.

Denton Record-Chronicle, January 31, 1971.

Ferguson, Henry N., "Enid Justin, Woman Bootmaker," Texas Woman, February 1979.

Roberts, O. M., "The Capitols of Texas," Texas State Historical Association Quarterly, II (October 1898).

Sparks, S. F., "Recollections of S. F. Sparks," Quarterly of the Texas State Historical Association, XII (July 1908).

Tascosa Pioneer, October 20, 1888.

### Letters

Doolittle, James H., Los Angeles, letter to author August 27, 1976.